THE U.S. ARMY COOKS' MANUAL

THE U.S. ARMY
COOKS' MANUAL

Edited by R. Sheppard

CASEMATE

Philadelphia & Oxford

Published in Great Britain and
the United States of America in 2018 by
CASEMATE PUBLISHERS
1950 Lawrence Road, Havertown, PA 19083, USA
The Old Music Hall, 106–108 Cowley Road, Oxford OX4 1JE, UK

© Casemate Publishers 2018

Hardback Edition: 978-1-61200-470-9
Digital Edition: 978-1-61200-471-6

All rights reserved. No part of this book may be reproduced or transmitted in any form or by
any means, electronic or mechanical including photocopying, recording or by any information storage and retrieval system, without permission from the publisher in writing.

A CIP record for this book is available from the British Library

Printed in the Czech Republic by FINIDR s.r.o.

For a complete list of Casemate titles, please contact:

CASEMATE PUBLISHERS (US)
Telephone (610) 853-9131
Fax (610) 853-9146
Email: casemate@casematepublishing.com
www.casematepublishing.com

CASEMATE PUBLISHERS (UK)
Telephone (01865) 241249
Fax (01865) 794449
Email: casemate-uk@casematepublishers.co.uk
www.casematepublishers.co.uk

Cover design by Katie Gabriel Allen.
Frontispiece: US Army in the trenches, World War I.

The recipes and instructions in this book are provided for information only. The publisher
assumes no responsibility of liability of any damage incurred resulting from following any of
the recipes or instructions printed in this book.

CONTENTS

INTRODUCTION

"The feeding of an army is a matter of the most vital importance, and demands the earliest attention of the general entrusted with the campaign."

General Sherman, *Memoirs*

"Food sustains the immense machinery of war"

John C. Calhoun, Secretary of War, 1817–25

N apoleon may or may not have actually uttered the immortal phrase "An army marches on its stomach," but any soldier will tell you it's true. Throughout history, an army with insufficient or inadequate food during a campaign is instantly at a huge disadvantage: the Roman writer Vegetius said that an army without supplies of grain and other provision exposed itself to defeat before even entering battle. In some cases, the outcome of a war could come down to which army had the better breakfast.

While a number of treatises on how to feed armies on the move appeared in several countries during the nineteenth century, it only tended to appear on a national political agenda when the existing system had completely failed the men flighting in the field e.g. when the British suffered from major supply issues in the Crimea. The introduction to *The Provisioning of the Modern Army in the Field* (1909) noted that: "The fact that in this country practically no books have been published on this important subject would seem to indicate that the public and the service are both indifferent to the matter, except spasmodically when attention is drawn to it by reports of suffering. Periods of peace afford no opportunities for practical experience, and indifference to a subject indicates lack of familiarity, and this because the incentive to study and preparation has not been made imperative."

Supplying the army at war had necessarily been a concern in America even before the declaration of independence, and Congress would approve several methods before a reliable system developed. As the nineteenth century progressed, the army was venturing farther afield, requiring supplies to be transported farther and preserved for longer, and by the turn of the twentieth century, the army was operating overseas in different climates, which offered further challenges. When food reached the men, it then had to be turned into palatable meals. When in camp for long periods of time the men might receive soft bread from the bakehouse, and meals from a field kitchen but most of the time in the field mealtimes meant huddles of tired men around camp fires, trying to create something edible (and safe) out of their rather uninspiring rations and with only limited utensils. Things came to a head during the Civil War when senior officers realized that the health of their men was being badly affected by their amateurish attempts at cooking. Manuals, and eventually training, followed, and the increased understanding of nutrition—and how soldiers could be provided with healthy and enticing meals in the garrison, in the field, and in transit—evident in the 1916 manual shows what progress had been made in just under a century and a half. The sophistication of the system would of course be taken to the next level in the following war.

This book does not pretend in any way to be a complete history of food in the U.S. Army (for some examples see the bibliography), but rather an insight into what they ate, the types of meals they cooked and how, through the manuals and reports produced by or for the U.S. Army.

CHAPTER I

FEEDING THE ARMY: 1775–1848

Feeding the Patriot soldiers in the field was of course a pressing concern for the Continental Congress, and a "commissary-general of stores and provisions" was created by resolution in 1775. The men were to be provided with a certain amount of food as a daily ration, yet could purchase other food and drink from the sutlers or other traders that accompanied the army. Out of necessity much of the ration was dried or salted, as was the military staple hardtack, a biscuit of flour and water that was cheap to make and long-lasting. But the best intentions of the Continental Congress were not enough to keep the men fed; soldiers did not receive their full ration complement, leaving them reliant on hunting, foraging, food parcels from home, and when desperate "liberating" provisions.

These early efforts of the commissary department met with so much dissatisfaction that there was an investigation by Congress in 1777, and a new system set up, with military agents purchasing the necessary provisions and ensuring these were delivered. Reforms then introduced forage masters, with contractors supplying rations to the mostly militia force. The new system was tested in the War of 1812, and it failed—troops on the Canadian frontier quickly ran short of rations as contractors failed to make deliveries. Though efforts were begun to improve the situation, a bill read in the Senate was postponed as peace took away the urgency and the matter of supplying the army was not considered again until the war against the Seminole Indians. The failure of contractors to supply rations in Georgia, despite having been

Detailed sketch by Arthur Lumley of the interior of a sutler's tent, with several full-length portraits of unidentified officers drinking at the bar, August 1862. Arthur Lumley. Sutlers would continue to offer soldiers the option of supplementing their army rations until 1866, when the office was abolished, and replaced with "post traders." (Library of Congress)

paid in advance, meant military movements were delayed, and by January 1818 the situation was desperate. After finding that the militia in Georgia had been released from service, partly due to lack of provisions, thus leaving the frontier exposed, General Jackson wrote to the Secretary of War, Hon. John C. Calhoun in February 1818:

> The mode of provisioning an army by contract is not adapted to the prompt and efficient movement of troops. It may answer in time of profound peace, where a failure or delay cannot produce any serious ill consequences; but where active operations are necessary, and success dependent on prompt and quick movements, there is no dependence to be placed on the contractor. His views are purely mercenary; and when supplies will not insure him a profit he hes-

itates not on a failure, never regarding how far it may defeat the best-devised plans of the Commander in Chief. Experience has confirmed me in this opinion, and the recent failure has prompted me again to express it.

His official report two weeks later related that "eleven hundred men are now here without a barrel of flour or bushel of corn. We have pork on foot; and to-morrow I shall proceed for Fort Scott, and endeavor to procure from the Indians a supply of corn that will aid in subsisting the detachment until we reach that place. How those failures have happened under the superintendence of regular officers I cannot imagine, but blame must rest somewhere, and it shall be strictly investigated as soon as circumstances will permit." General Jackson took matters into his own hands, and having managed to acquire supplies, he began a successful campaign against the Seminoles. This debacle led to requests in the Senate for full information about the rationing and provisioning of the army. A report covering Army and Army Staff organization by Calhoun covered in detail the quality of army rations.

Reduction of the Army Considered

Communicated to the House of Representatives, December 14, 1818

On the quality of the ration, and the system of supplying and issuing it, which I propose next to consider, the health, comfort, and efficiency of the Army mainly depend. Too much care cannot be bestowed on these important subjects; for let the military system be ever so perfect in other particulars, any considerable deficiency in these must, in all great military operations, expose an army to the greatest disasters. All human efforts must, of necessity, be limited by the means of sustenance. Food sustains the immense machinery of war, and gives the impulse to all its operations; and if this essential be withdrawn, even but for a few days, the whole must cease to act. No absolute standard can be fixed, as regards either quantity or quality of the ration. These must vary, according to the habits and products of different countries. The great objects are, first, and mainly, to sustain the health and spirit of the troops; and the next, to do it with the least possible expense. The system which effects these in the greatest degree is the most perfect. The ration, as established by the act of the 16th March, 1802, experience proves to be ample in quantity, but not of the quality best calculated to secure either health or economy. It consists of eighteen ounces of bread or flour; one pound and a quarter of beef, or three-quarters of a pound of pork; one gill of rum, brandy, or whisky; and at the rate of two quarts of salt, four quarts of vinegar, four pounds of soap, and one pound and a half of candles, to every hundred rations.

Our people, even the poorest, being accustomed to a plentiful mode of living, require, to preserve their health, a continuation, in a considerable degree, of the same habits of life, in a camp; and a sudden and great departure from it subjects them, as is proved by experience, to great mortality. Our losses, in the late and Revolutionary wars, from this cause, were probably greater than from the sword. However well qualified for war in other respects, in the mere capacity of bearing privations we are inferior to most nations. An American would starve on what a Tartar would live with comfort. In fact, barbarous and oppressed nations have, in this particular, a striking advantage, which, however, ought to be much more than compensated by the skill and resources of a free and civilized people. If, however, such a people want the skill and spirit to direct its resources to its defense, the very wealth, by which it ought to defend itself, becomes the motive for invasion and conquest. Besides, there is something shocking to the feelings, that in a country of plenty beyond all others, in a country which ordinarily is so careful of the happiness and life of the meanest of its citizens, that its brave defenders, who are not only ready, but anxious to expose their lives for the safety and glory of their country, should, through a defective system of supply, be permitted almost to starve, or to perish by the poison of unwholesome food, as has frequently been the case. If it could be supposed that these considerations are not sufficient to excite the most anxious care on this subject, we ought to remember, that nothing adds more to the expense of military operations, or exposes more to its disasters, than the sickness and mortality which result from defective or unwholesome supplies. Impressed with this view of the subject, considerable changes have been made in the ration, under the authority of the eighth section of the act regulating the Staff of the Army, passed at the last session of Congress. The vegetable part of the ration has been much increased. Twice a week, a half allowance of meat, with a suitable quantity of peas or beans, is directed to be issued. Fresh meat has also been substituted twice a week for salted. In the Southern Division, bacon and kiln-dried Indian corn-meal have been, to a certain extent, substituted for pork and wheat flour. In addition, orders have been given, at all of the permanent posts where it can be done, to cultivate a sufficient supply of ordinary garden vegetables for the use of the troops; and at the posts remote from the settled parts of the country, the order is extended to the cultivation of corn and to the supply of the meat part of the ration, both to avoid the expense of distant and expensive transportation and to secure at all times a supply within the posts themselves.

In addition to these changes, I am of opinion that the spirit part of the ration, as a regular issue, ought to be dispensed with; and such appears to be the opinion of most of the officers of the Army. It both produces and perpetuates habits of intemperance, destructive alike to the health, and moral and physical energy of the soldiers. The spirits ought to be placed in depot, and be issued occasionally under the direction of the commander. Thus used, their noxious effects would be avoided, and the troops, when great efforts were necessary, would, by a judicious use, derive important benefits therefrom. Molasses, beer, and cider, according to circumstances, might be used as substitutes. The substitution of bacon and kiln-dried corn-meal in the Southern Division will have, it is believed, valuable effects. They are both much more congenial to the habit of the people in that section of our country. Corn-meal has another, and,

15

in my opinion, great and almost decisive advantage—it requires so little art to prepare it for use. It is not easy to make good bread of wheat flour, whilst it is almost impossible to make bad of that of Indian corn; besides, wheat is much more liable to be damaged than the Indian corn; for the latter is better protected against disease, and the effects of bad seasons in time of harvest than any other grain; and, when injured, the good is easily separated from the bad. Experience proves it to be not less nutritious than wheat, or any other grain. Parched corn constitutes the principal food of an Indian warrior; and such are its nutritious qualities, that they can support long and fatiguing marches on it alone.

I next proceed to consider the system of supplying the Army with provisions, or the establishment of a commissariat; and, as they are connected in their nature, I propose to consider that part of the resolution in relation to a commissariat, and the mode of issuing the rations at the same time. The system established at the last session will, in time of peace, be adequate to the cheap and certain supply of the Army. The act provides for the appointment of a Commissary-General, and as many Assistants as the service may require, and authorizes the President to assign to them their duties in purchasing and issuing rations. It also directs that the ordinary supplies of the Army should be purchased on contracts, to be made by the Commissary-General, and to be delivered, on inspection, in the bulk, at such places as shall be stipulated in the contract.

The Subsistence Department, under a Commissary-General, was created in 1818, responsible for acquiring, inspecting, and delivering supplies to units. As the department proved better than previous systems it was made permanent, and the number of men working in it increased to allow it to support the army in wartime.

At this time, soldiers tended to cook in messes of six to 12, using communal kettles and mess tins—they would have to be resourceful if the wagons carrying the utensils hadn't caught up with them when it was approaching time for dinner. The 1821 Army Regulations had a few comments on Messing, though how useful soldiers found these instructions (or whether they paid them any heed at all) is debatable.

General Regulations for the Army

Article 27: Messing

Bread and soup are the great items of a soldier's diet in every situation: to make them well is, therefore, an essential part of his instruction. Those great scourges of a camp life, the scurvy and diarrhoea, more frequently result from a want of skill in cooking, than from the badness of the ration, or from any other cause whatever. Officers in command, and more immediately regimental officers, will therefore give a strict attention to this vital branch of interior economy, with a view to which, as well as to multiply their resources in time of siege or scarcity, they will do well to read the articles "Baking," and "Bread," in the different Encyclopaedias.

Bread ought not to be burnt, but baked to an equal brown colour. The crust ought not to be detached from the crum. On opening it, when fresh, one ought to smell a sweet and balsamic odour.

In making biscuits or hard bread, the evaporation is about fifty-four pounds, so that the barrel of flour yields but one hundred and eighty-two pounds of biscuits. Double-baked bread loses, in like manner, about ninety-five pounds, and keeps much longer than that which is singly baked.

The troops ought not to be allowed to eat soft bread fresh from the oven, without first toasting it. This process renders it nearly as wholesome and nutritious as stale bread.

Fresh meat ought not to be cooked before it has had time to bleed and to cool; and meats will generally be boiled, with a view to soup; sometimes roasted or baked, but never fried.

Fresh meat issued to the soldiers in advance, in hot weather, may be preserved by half boiling it; or, if there be not time for that operation, the meat may be kept some twenty-four hours, by previously exposing it, for a few minutes, to a very thick smoke.

To make soup, put into the vessel at the rate of five pints of water to a pound of fresh meat; apply a quick heat, to make it boil promptly; skim off the foam, and then moderate the fire; salt is then put in, according to the palate. Add the vegetables of the season one or two hours, and sliced bread some minutes before the simmering is ended. When the broth is sensibly reduced in quantity, that is, after five or six hours' cooking, the process will be complete.

If a part of the meat is to be withdrawn before the soup is fully made, the quantity of water will be proportionably less. Hard or dry vegetables will be put in earlier than is above indicated.

The choice of water for bread, soup, or for boiling vegetables, is essential. As far as practicable, limpid water, without scent or peculiar taste, and which dissolves soap freely, only will be used. River or rain water is preferable to that of springs, wells or ponds. Hard or dry vegetables, as pulse and rice, cannot be well cooked in water that rests on, or passes over, calcareous earths.

Vinegar, particularly in hot weather, is essential to the soldier's mess. Great care will be taken to procure that which is of a good quality; and the surgeons will frequently be consulted on the subject of this article, as on every other interesting to the health of the troops.

Messes will be prepared by privates of squads, including private musicians, each taking his tour; and the greatest care will be observed in scouring and washing the utensils employed in cooking. Those made of brass or copper will not be used, unless, in the case of copper, the vessel be well lined with tin.

While the Mexican War (1846–48) strained the army's resources—being the first time the army had sustained operations outside of the United States—it overcame difficulties and was able to meet the logistics demands. After the end of the Mexican War the United States reached ocean to ocean—taxing the energies of the Subsistence and Quartermaster departments as they constantly had to transport supplies over vast distances, mainly by wagon or mule train. Some posts had to lay in months of supplies because they were thousands of miles from the closest depots. This meant of course that food might well be spoiled by the time it was issued to the troops. Even if it arrived relatively fresh, the soldiers faced the unrelenting monotony of coffee, hardtack and bacon at most every meal, as there was little food available locally to supplement the ration. In some areas hunting might increase variety, and at some posts gardens could provide fresh vegetables at least part of the year. Contact with Indian tribes introduced the soldiers to some new types of food, such as pemmican—which would later be included in the *Manual for Army Cooks*.

CHAPTER 2

CREATING SOLDIER COOKS:
1848–1898

Despite their best efforts, neither the Union nor the Confederate army completely solved the problem of food supply during the Civil War. The Union Army started with the advantage of an established Subsistence Department of the regular army, which by the end of the war had grown to 564 officers. Abraham Lincoln commented to an officer of the Subsistence Department in Richmond in 1865: "Your Department we scarcely hear of. It is like a well-regulated stomach: works so smoothly that we are not conscious of having it." In his annual report for 1865, the Secretary of War, Hon. Edwin M. Stanton said, "During the war this branch of the service never failed. It answers to the demand, and is ever ready to meet the national call."

The ration was set out in the United States Army regulations of 1861:

A ration is the established daily allowance of food for one person. For the United States army it is composed as follows: twelve ounces of pork or bacon, or, one pound and four ounces of salt or fresh beef; one pound and six ounces of soft bread or flour, or, one pound of hard bread, or, one pound and four ounces of corn meal; and to every one hundred rations, fifteen pounds of beans or peas, and ten pounds of rice or hominy; ten pounds of green coffee, or, eight pounds of roasted (or roasted and ground) coffee, or, one pound and eight ounces of tea; fifteen pounds of sugar; four quarts of vinegar; one pound and four ounces of adamantine or star candles; four pounds of soap; three pounds and twelve ounces of salt; four ounces of pepper; thirty pounds of potatoes, when practicable, and one quart of molasses. The Subsistence Department, as may be most convenient or least expensive to it, and according to the condition and amount of its supplies, shall determine whether soft bread or flour, and what other component parts of the ration, as equivalents, shall be issued. Desiccated compressed potatoes, or desiccated compressed mixed vegetables, at the rate of one ounce and a half of the former, and one ounce of the latter, to the ration, may be substituted for beans, peas, rice, hominy, or fresh potatoes.

As had long been the case, soldiers in the field would cook in small messes, and there is far less guidance than in earlier regulations on how to cook their rations: "The bread must be thoroughly baked, and not eaten until it is cold. The soup must be boiled at least five hours, and the vegetables always cooked sufficiently to be perfectly soft and digestible." As many units, North and South, comprised solely fresh-faced volunteers who had never cooked a meal in their life, many a soldier was destined to spend the war complaining about insufficient food badly cooked in haste over camp fires by untrained cooks, often with quite limited equipment (or no equipment).

The problem did not go unnoticed by senior officers, who realized the effect it was having on the men's health. James Sanderson, a hotel operator and a member of the newly formed United States Sanitary Commission, took an experienced cook and visited troops in the field to test out a simple system of cookery. The day after the battle of Bull Run, Sanderson suggested to the War Department a system of appointing a skilled cook to each regiment who would

"Reinforcements for our volunteers on the march southward," *Harper's Weekly* (June 1861).

THE FOOD QUESTION DOWN SOUTH.

Jeff Davis. "See! see! the beautiful Boots just come to me from the dear ladies of Baltimore!"

Beauregard. "Ha! Boots? Boots? When shall we eat them? Now?"

Editorial cartoon shows Jefferson Davis, president of the Confederate states, offering a new pair of boots to General Beauregard who, though barefoot, would rather have food for his troops. *Harper's Weekly* (May 1863). (Library of Congress)

then teach other men to become cooks. Not all of his recommendations were followed, but he was commissioned in office of the commissary general, and then wrote the first cook book for soldiers, *Camp Fires and Camp Cooking*, for the Army of the Potomac. This short book includes recipes for various stews, soups, beans, bread in portable field ovens, and instructions on cooking bacon, potatoes, rice and how to prepare the all-important coffee, which was at this time provided to soldiers as green beans, requiring roasting and grinding before they could finally be used to brew coffee.

Fall in for soup, company mess. E. Forbes, "Life Studies of the great army," c. 1876. (Morgan collection of Civil War drawings, Library of Congress)

Camp Fires and Camp Cooking or Culinary Hints for the Soldier

By Captain James M. Sanderson

Published for distribution to the Troops. Headquarters "Army of the Potomac," January, 1862.

In making up the following receipts, the author has been actuated by a desire to aid the efforts of those of his countrymen who, with the best intentions, lack the knowledge to utilize them; and having personally assisted in the concoction of the various dishes he treats of, using only camp fires, camp kettles, and soldiers' rations, he knows that a little attention on the part of any sensible man—and none other should ever attempt to cook—will produce the most savory and gratifying results.

CAMP COOKING AND CAMP KETTLES.

The utensils and means furnished by government to the soldier for preparing his food are of the most primitive character. The former consists of camp kettles, made of iron, with a handle, and varying in size from four to seven gallons, (they should be made so as to have one slide into the other, in nests of four) and mess pans, also of iron, about 12 inches in diameter, and sloping to the bottom. The latter consist of a certain amount of wood per diem, which is to be consumed as taste or ingenuity may dictate. The usual and most simple mode is to dig a trench 18 inches wide, 12 inches deep, and from four to six feet long. At each end plant a forked stick of equal height, with a stout sapling, from which to suspend the kettles, extending from one to the other.

This, however, is neither the best nor most economical mode, as it consumes much fuel, wastes much of the heat, and causes great inconvenience to the cook. An improvement can be effected by casing the sides of the trench with brick, adding a little chimney at one end, and, in place of the forked sticks, using iron uprights and cross-bar, to which half a dozen hooks for hanging kettles are attached.

In a clayey soil, the plan adopted by the salt boilers of New York is perhaps the neatest, most economical, and most convenient that can be devised. They dig a hole about three feet square and two feet in depth, generally in the slope of a hill. On one side they run a shaft laterally, about one foot square and six feet in length, and one foot from the surface of the ground. At the extreme end they sink a shaft vertically, and form a chimney; and at equi-distances they pierce three holes of sufficient diameter to prevent the kettles from slipping through. By this mode the kettles can be placed over the fire to boil—or on either side, to simmer—with less difficulty than by any other means.

Besides the allowance from government, however, the company cooks should be furnished, from the "Company Fund," with two large iron spoons, two large iron forks, two stout knives, one tin cullender, and one yard of flannel; also a false tin bottom, closely fitting the kettles; for all of which the cook should be responsible.

THE RATION.

No army in the world is so well provided for, in the shape of food, either as to quantity or quality, as the army of the United States, and very little attention on the part of the cook will enable him to lay up a liberal amount weekly to the credit of the Company Fund. No one man can consume his daily ration, although men waste it; and a systematic issue will, in a great measure, prevent unnecessary extravagance.

THE COOK'S CREED.

Cleanliness is next to godliness, both in persons and kettles: be ever industrious, then, in scouring your pots. Much elbow grease, a few ashes, and a little water, are capital aids to the careful cook. Better wear out your pans with scouring than your stomachs with purging; and it is less dangerous to work your elbows than your comrade's bowels. Dirt and grease betray the poor cook, and destroy the poor soldier; whilst health, content, and good cheer should ever reward him who does his duty and keeps his kettles clean. In military life, punctuality is not only a duty, but a necessity, and the cook should always endeavor to be exact in time. Be sparing with sugar and salt, as a deficiency can be better remedied than an overplus.

KITCHEN PHILOSOPHY.

Remember that beans, badly boiled, kill more than bullets; and fat is more fatal than powder. In cooking, more than in anything else in this world, always make haste slowly. One hour too much is vastly better than five minutes too little, with rare exceptions. A big fire scorches your soup, burns your face, and crisps your temper. Skim, simmer, and scour, are the true secrets of good cooking.

BEEF SOUP WITH DESICCATED MIXED VEGETABLES.

The Americans, as a rule, are not fond of soups, unless of the thicker kind; but in no form can meat and vegetables be served together more profitably and more nourishingly. As a matter of economy, it admits of no argument, because every portion is useful, both bone and flesh; and, when properly made, it is wholesome and palatable. On fresh-beef day, if among the rations there are some choice bits—such as sirloin, tenderloin, or rump steaks—cut them into neat slices, and use for breakfast, broiling them if it can be done; if not, fry them. Save all the bones, if large cut them in pieces and distribute equally among the kettles. If the company numbers seventy men or less, use one large kettle and two smaller ones. Fill them nearly with pieces of meat, from one to three pounds each, not too closely packed; then add water enough to cover it, and place it over a brisk fire, throwing in a large handful of salt to each kettle.

"The way they cook dinner in camp," Army of the Potomac.

As soon as the water begins to boil, and the scum begins to rise, deaden the fire, and skim, carefully and faithfully, every ten minutes, and be very sure that the water does not again come to a boil—*it should only simmer*; for when the meat is boiling hard the pores of the flesh are immediately closed, the essence of the meat, and all its impurities, are retained within, no scum arises, the meat becomes hard and tough, and the soup thin and watery. If it is only permitted to simmer, the pores are kept open, the blood is drawn out, the juices are extracted, the meat is rendered tender and wholesome, and the soup rich, nutritious, and palatable. In one hour and a half—carefully skimming all the while—the meat should be done; but if it has only simmered, two hours will be better. Then take the meat out, leaving only the bones. An hour previous to this, however, break up a tablet of desiccated vegetables as small as possible, and divide them into as many portions as there are kettles of soup. Place each portion in a separate pan, and fill with fresh clean water, standing them near the fire until thoroughly saturated with water. When the meat is taken out, put the vegetables in, and let them boil gently two hours longer, during that time carefully skimming off all the fat which rises to the surface. Then season with pepper and salt, and a tablespoonful of vinegar, and serve out.

Both the French and American desiccated vegetables come in tablets. The former being twice as large as the latter, it will therefore be necessary to use one of the French or two of the American tablets for a company, which will be found amply sufficient, as they swell up to sixteen times their bulk in a compressed state.

Sanderson assumes that the cook will always have his equipment to hand, but this was not always the case for either the Union or the Confederate soldier, as explained by E. N. Horsford in his pamphlet *The Army Ration* of 1864:

> The soldier carries his plate, fork, and spoon in his haversack, his canteen is slung over the shoulder with his haversack, and his cup is made fast to his knapsack or belt. The kettles, frying-pans and bake-pans are sometimes carried by men detailed for the purpose, but more frequently in the regimental wagon, or on the backs of mules; and on the march are often a long distance in the rear. They are sometimes captured or lost. After the fatigue of a long march or the sufferings of an engagement, they are, in the latter case more especially, almost certain as a matter of safety to be a long distance from the point where they can be of service. From the time the Army of the Potomac left Falmouth through all the march to Gettysburg and back to Brandy Station—a whole campaign—the camp-kettles in some regiments were not once brought into service.

While other guides and manuals followed Sanderson's for the Union soldier, none seems to have been produced for Confederate soldiers, who were perhaps more concerned with the supply of rations than the niceties of cooking it; Confederate rations were reduced several times during the war. There were also fewer sutlers with the South to which a soldier might turn to supplement his rations with, if indeed he *could* afford to. There were shortages of foodstuffs, including the all-important coffee. Trading along the lines was common when men were on picket duty, tobacco in exchange for coffee for example. Confederate cooks similarly suffered without utensils, and they had no Sanderson to give them hints.

In the years after the Civil War, the problems of military food supply and preparation would not be completely forgotten. The Surgeon-General's *Report on the Hygiene of the United States Army* (1875) concluded that rations were insufficient and deficient, in particular failing to provide the men with vegetables. He noted that "to keep men in good condition, there should be not only abundance but variety, and the want of this is due partly to the ration itself, and partly to the limited knowledge of different modes of preparing food possessed by the cooks." Among his recommendations to improve the food supply of the army (and therefore the health of the men), was a suggestion that the chief cook of each company be a permanent detail—cooks were at this time still rotated every ten days but this was for obvious reasons mainly disregarded in the case of the chief cook. It was

The Soldiers sharing rations

Soldiers sharing rations, Appomattox Campaign, 1865. Written on the reverse: "The rebel soldiers were entirely without food and our men shared coffee and rations with them." Alfred R. Waud. (Morgan collection of Civil War drawings, Library of Congress)

noted that the position of company cook was not particularly desired, so extra-duty pay was recommended. It was further suggested that cooks be specially enlisted for that duty. Finally, it was recommended that a school for the instruction of cooks would be established at the recruiting depots, and that a manual of instruction for army cooks be prepared and issued by the Subsistence department.

While a permanent position of cook was not established until 1898, and formal training began even later, a suitable manual was prepared relatively quickly. In 1877, a board of officers was convened to study food preparation, trials and recommend recipes, which were then published as the *Manual for Army Cooks* in 1879. This manual would be revised over several editions during the next thirty-odd years.

By the time it was in its fourth edition, the manual had been much expanded and was now arranged in two parts, 'The Army Ration in Garrison', and 'Camp Cookery'. In Part I there were detailed bills of fare for a certain number of weeks, and detailed information on Army Range, No. 4 (a stove and oven system), whereas Part II offered a variety of ways to cook while in the field, and included a surprisingly wide range of recipes.

Camp cooks at work, Civil War. Mathew Brady. (NARA)

Manual for Army Cooks

1896

Part II: CAMP COOKERY

Camp Cookery may be divided into three kinds: Permanent Camps, Temporary Camps, and on a continuous march.

The principles are the same in each kind, the differences being only as to the conveniences that are at hand in each case.

The appetite of men taken from quarters and placed in the field increases considerably for the first few days. Meats that would be indigestible from toughness, and simple dishes often neglected while living in barracks, are eaten with appetite.

COOKING PLACES.

Each company should have its own kitchen on flank of, and in line with, its row of tents. The simplest kitchen consists of a trench dug in the direction parallel with the wind, of such width that the kettle, when placed on it, does not project beyond it more than an inch on each side; its depth should be 12 inches at the end from which the wind is blowing, and continue this depth for 4 feet, decreasing then gradually to 3 inches at the opposite end, where a space must be left equal to the breadth of the trench, to serve as a chimney. The fire is lit at the end where the trench is deep; it should not extend beyond 3 or 4 feet up the trench. The kettles are placed touching one another; dry sods should be used to stop up the chinks made by the roundness of the kettles, so that the space under them may form a flue. It is advisable to pile up sod, or, with stones and earth, to erect a chimney of at least one foot in height at the end farthest from the fire. All grass around the fireplaces should be cut to prevent accidents from fire.

If the command halts for more than one day, these kitchens are susceptible of great improvement; the chimney can be made of mud, or twigs and mud, and the draft may be increased by using short pieces of hoop iron as bars, stretched across the trench to support a filling in of clay around each kettle; or, in other words, to make a regular place for each kettle, into which it will fit exactly, so that its position may be changed. As the day following the wind may change to an exactly opposite direction, a similar trench must be dug in continuation of the former one, the same chimney being used. In this manner one chimney will serve for trenches cut to suit the wind blowing from all four quarters. The openings from these trenches into the chimney must all be closed with sod, except the one in use. In some places, where bricks or stones suitable to the purpose are to be had, it is better to construct these kitchens on the ground instead of below the surface.

In well-wooded countries, two logs side by side and parallel to the direction of the wind, the fire being kindled between them, make a good kitchen. In such places fuel is no object, so the construction of chimneys can be dispensed with, and the kettles hung from a stick resting at each end on a forked upright.

HOW TO MAKE A COOKING FIRE FOR A SMALL CAMP.

Lay down two green poles (5 by 6 inches thick, and 2 feet long) 2 or 3 feet apart, with notches in the upper side about 10 to 12 inches apart. Let the ground be leveled meantime. Take two more green poles (6 by 8 inches thick, and 4 feet long) and lay them in the notches. Procure a good supply of dry wood, bark, brush, or chips, and start your fire on the ground between the poles. The air will circulate under and through your fire, and the poles are just the right distance apart to set your camp kettle, frying pan, or coffee pot on.

If you are going to cook several meals in this place, it will pay you to put up a crane. This is built as follows: Cut two green posts (2 inches thick and 3 feet long), which drive into the ground a foot from either end of your fire, and then split the top end of each with the ax (unless they be forked).

Then cut another green pole, of same size, and long enough to reach from one of these posts to the other; flatten the ends and insert them in the splits. The posts should be of such height that when this pole is passed through the bail of the camp kettle, the latter will swing just clear of the fire. Other cooking utensils may be used as required.

DISPOSAL OF REFUSE.

Particular attention is directed to the cleanly method of burning all kitchen refuse in the camp fire; it will not affect the cooking. Burn everything—coffee grounds, parings, bones, meats, even old tin cans, for if thrown out anywhere, even buried, they attract flies. Tin cans are flytraps—-burned and cleaned out of fire daily they are harmless. Fires, should be cleaned of burnt refuse once a day, as refuse burned will not attract flies; Cleanliness is a good doctor. The burning of refuse, not burying it, is a splendid rule, especially in a large command or permanent camp.

EXTEMPORIZED STOVES, OR COOKING PLACE.

(With Plates.)

In the field the utensils furnished are of primitive character, consisting of camp kettles and mess pans, made of iron, etc.

To extemporize stoves and cooking places the usual and most simple mode is to dig a trench 18 inches wide, 12 inches deep, and from 4 to 6 feet long. At each end place a forked stick, of equal height, with a stout sapling, from which to suspend the kettles, extending from one to the other. (See plate 1.)

This, however, is neither the best nor most economical mode, as it consumes much fuel, wastes much of the heat, and causes great inconvenience

PLATE 1.

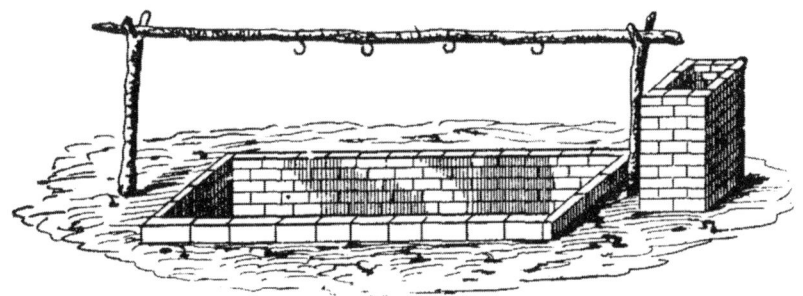

PLATE 2.

35

to the cook. An improvement can be effected by casing the sides of the trench with brick, adding a little chimney at one end, and, in place of the forked sticks, using iron uprights and crossbar, to which half a dozen hooks for hanging kettles are attached. (See plate 2.)

In a clayey soil, the following plan is perhaps the neatest, most economical, and most convenient that can be devised: Dig a hole about 3 feet square and 2 feet in depth, generally in the slope of a hill. On one side run a shaft laterally, about 1 foot square and 6 feet in length, and 1 foot from the surface of the ground. At the extreme end sink a shaft vertically, and form a chimney; and at equidistances pierce three holes of sufficient diameter to prevent the kettles from slipping through. By this mode kettles can be placed over the fire to boil—or on either side, to simmer—with less difficulty than by any other means. (See plate 3.)

SHIELD FOR CAMP FIRE.

Made of light boiler or heavy sheet iron. Composed of top and three sides, joined to top by hinges.

Fuel is inserted in front, which should be to the windward, and being open, any length of wood can be used. One joint of pipe is sufficient.

This is very portable, and in windy weather a comfort for the cooks and those who would gather around the camp fire. (See plates 5 and 6.)

BUZZACOTT OVEN.

Various portable stoves and ovens have been invented and placed upon the market for use in camp cookery.

The Buzzacott oven is now generally used in the Army; it is an adaptation from the Dutch oven. It consists of a large rectangular box; the bottom is made of sheet iron or steel, with a top of similar material.

It is compact and strong for transportation.

The outfit includes all the necessary utensils for roasting, baking, frying, broiling, and stewing, as well as many of the cooks' tools for the use of a full company of seventy-five men. It is issued by the Quartermaster's Department, upon requisition, to United States troops, for use in field and camp service.

Plate 7 represents the entire military outfit, as packed for transportation. Inside are the thirty to thirty-five utensils comprising the outfit. Size, 25 by 35 by 14 inches. Weight, 175 to 200 lbs., complete. In shipping, it forms its own crate, and when thus closed this skeleton stove forms an iron crate about

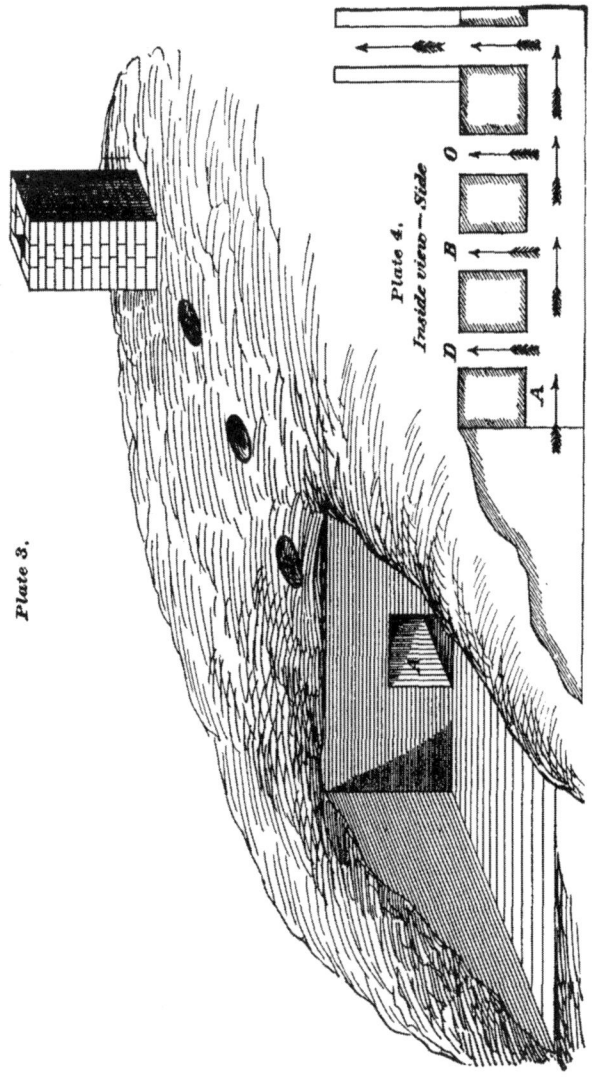

Plate 3.

Plate 4.
Inside view — Side

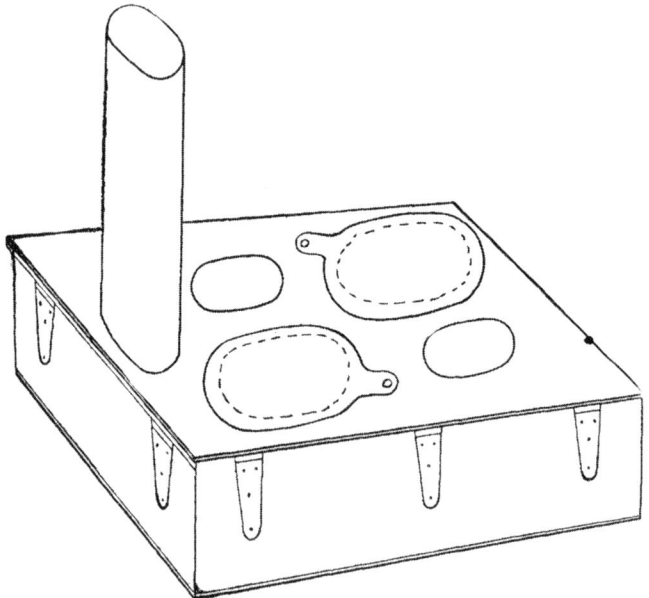

PLATE 5.—Dimensions Length, 30 inches; width, 26 inches; height, 12 inches.

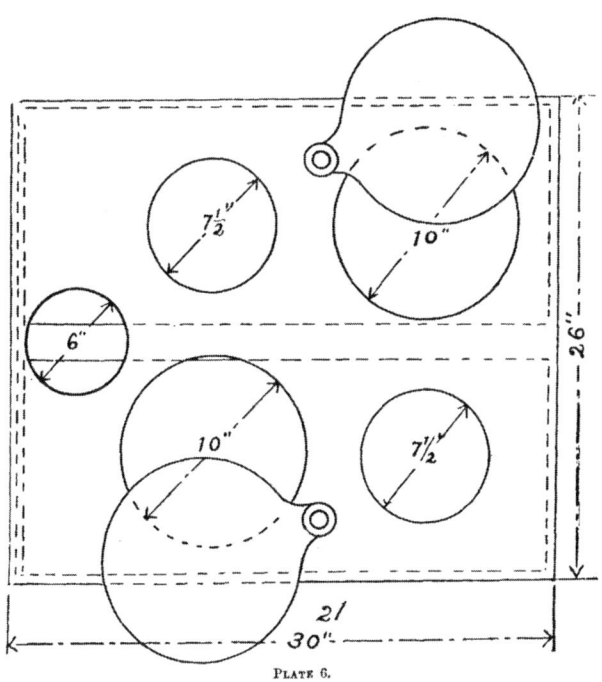

PLATE 6.

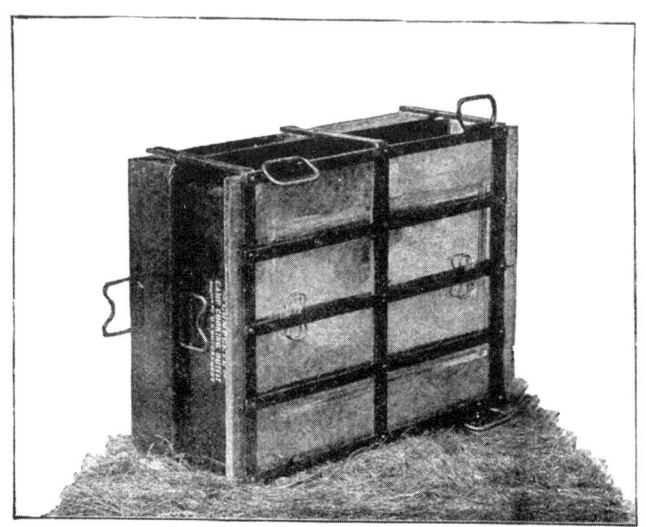

PLATE 7.

PLATE 8.

the whole, fastens or binds it together and permits of any heavy objects being packed on top of it without danger of crushing.

Plate 8 represents the general appearance when set up for use. It can, however, be rearranged as circumstances require.

WHAT THE OUTFIT COMPRISES.

One skeleton stove (grate stand).

One extension stand.

Two parts of oven.

One large cover for oven (used when boiling water, etc.).

Two large baking and roasting spiders. Rests.

Two small frying spiders. Rests.

Two lifting hooks or irons.

Two large combination frying, roasting, or baking pans, with covers.

Three large boilers (a set), with covers to fit.

These articles are of special make, handmade, and of selected material, permitting of the rough and constant usage incident to field service.

UTENSILS PACKED WITH THE OUTFIT.

One butcher cleaver, 8-inch blade.

One butcher knife, 8-inch blade.

One butcher steel, 10-inch.

One 10-quart (seamless) dish or mixing pan.

One large sieve or strainer.

One large 10-quart dipper, handle 12 inches long.

One medium cup-dipper or ladle, handle 12 inches long.

One large cook's spoon, solid handle, 12 inches long.

One large cook's flesh fork, 3-prong, handle 12 inches long.

Three large dredges (salt, pepper, flour).

One large pierced ladle or skimmer.

One graduated scoop or measure, ½ pint to 2 quarts.

One large seamless colander.

One large turnover, solid handle, 12 inches long.

CAPACITY OF UTENSILS.

The largest boiler, full measure, 12 gallons, 48 quarts.

The medium boiler, full measure, 10 gallons, 40 quarts.

The smallest boiler, full measure, 8 gallons, 32 quarts.

Combined capacity, full measure, 30 gallons, 120 quarts.

Largest pan, baking (1 time), 100 biscuits, 30 pounds bread.

Medium pan, baking (1 time), 75 biscuits, 25 pounds bread.

Largest pan, roasting (1 time), 75 to 100 pounds meat.

Largest pan, frying (1 time), 75 to 100 pounds meat, fish, etc.

Largest pan, baking and roasting together, 50 pounds potatoes and 50 pounds meats.

Largest pan, baking beans, pudding, etc., 35 to 40 pounds.

If oven is used as a boiler, 10 to 15 hams can be boiled together in it, or one barrel of liquid prepared. In an emergency only is this necessary.

DIRECTIONS FOR USING BUZZACOTT OVEN.

If the wind is blowing heavily dig a hole for the oven and fire of sufficient depth to bring the top of the oven on a level with ground, piling the wood on the edges of the bank for additional protection. If weather is good there is no need of this.

When practicable use a tent fly as a shade for the cooks.

Use the best fuel for baking, and stack it so that it may dry. Splitting or chopping wood is not required, except to first kindle fire.

Build a fire of any convenient fuel, wood, buffalo chips, leaves (anything), and when well started, place over the fire your skeleton stove.

Adjust the "extension stand" always to leeward (from the wind), so as to catch or absorb the spare and draft heat, flame, etc.; use the "oven" on this stand, and shift the stand as circumstances require for your convenience.

When roasting or baking is desired in connection with boiling or frying, place the oven on the stand crosswise, as that allows room for the other utensils at the same time; or if preferable, place it on a bed of coals near the fire on the ground, or on a level fire.

Near the center of the inside of the oven place evenly apart the two large pan spiders (rests). These support the baking and roasting pans and contents and prevent an uneven circulation. Place these firmly and easily, and your foods will roast and bake splendidly.

Prepare the roast, bread, pudding, or whatever you wish in the pan, place it on the rests inside of the oven and cover with the upper part of the oven; heap some fresh burning coals on top and the roasting or baking commences instantly.

In using the oven keep a clean fire, free from sand and dirt. On top of oven build a little fire, if necessary, from chips, etc.; regulate your heat by the amount of fire—add to or remove when necessary.

Always build a fire or use live coals on top of the oven when either roasting or baking.

The two smaller pan spiders (rests) are intended to be used on top of the oven, over the fire that is built on top. On this do your boiling, stewing, broiling, and frying with the utensils (provided with the outfit) for the purpose.

Keep the oven covered as much as possible.

Basting is never required; to regulate the heat simply shift the fire, add to or remove as necessary; judge cooking by time and strength of fire; add water to the roasts for gravy, etc., and to assist its self-basting qualities.

When roasting or baking is completed, take off the oven, remove the cover and dump the ashes; recover it, and you can carry the oven and its contents clean and warm, being careful to avoid spilling or capsizing the food.

When removing pans with lifters, be careful to steady contents and lift easily, lest they capsize and spill contents.

Use the oven for washing dishes, and the top for frying and stewing (in addition to regular frying pan if desired).

The washing of pots, kettles, etc., will be easy if they are washed immediately, after use—before they cool—it will be done in one-half the time with one-quarter the work. Set them bottom up to drain and keep clean.

THE BARNEY STEAM COOKER AND STERILIZER.

The Barney Steam Cooker and Sterilizer operates under the principle of a complete circulation of steam. No water from condensation can come in contact with the food. It has been tested that onions, cabbage, fish, pudding, etc., can be cooked at the same time without taint or odor. As a sterilizer it is invaluable. No adulteration of food; no harmful germs. Requires no special attention. Can be used on gas, oil, coal, or wood stoves.

The 18 by 24 Barney Steam Cooker is composed of two sections—kettle rest and roasting pan; the sections are known as the bottom and top sections, and are made of the No. 24 galvanized sheet steel; the cover is made of the same material. The kettle is made of the best two-cross charcoal tin and has a

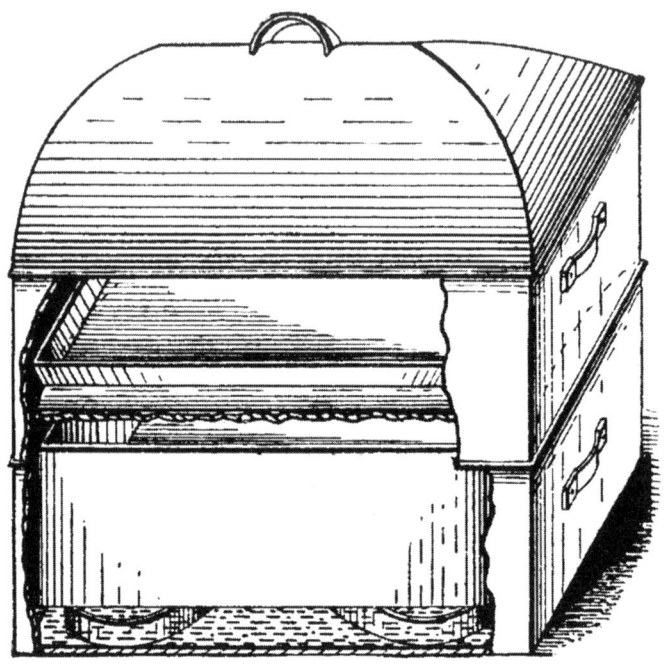

PLATE 9.
No. 1, Army ; size, 18 by 24 inches ; weight, 100 pounds.

capacity of 13 gallons of liquid substance, meaning 120 plates of soup or 160 cups of coffee, and will hold rations of vegetables for 100 men. The baking pan is made of No. 27 black iron, is 16½ by 21½ by 4¼ inches deep; this means a capacity of 75 pounds of roast beef. All food to be cooked in the Barney Steam Cooker is prepared the same as when cooked by the old method. The circular will give the desired information as to how the food is prepared and cooked in the steamer.

INSTRUCTIONS FOR USING THE COOKER.

Fill the bottom with water to the top of rest on which the kettle sits; no more water will be required for 3 to 4 hours over a moderate fire; should the time necessitate, the cooker may be placed over a hot fire, only being careful to keep a supply of water in the bottom; other than this no watch or care is necessary. In making soup and liquid food there should be no more water used than is required to serve, as there is no boiling away of the water in the kettles. The reason of this is that, the heat being equal on all sides of the kettles, there is no evaporation; so it has been proved that 10 gallons of water, placed in the kettles and steamed over a hot fire for 10 hours, when again measured was found to be still 10 gallons. The water in the bottom of the steamer being directly in contact with the raw heat the gases will naturally be consumed, and so of course will have to be replenished after 3 or 4 hours.

For boiling rice, hominy, oatmeal, etc., just enough water is added to allow their kernels or substance to swell.

The stove is operated by first putting the legs or supports together and fastening them to the stove by placing them in the sockets prepared to receive them; if convenient there should be a small hole or ditch dug for the fire (although this is not necessary). The stove is then placed over the place thus prepared and a fire kindled, using wood broken or cut three feet or less in length, or any material that will make a good fire.

The cooking should be done in a sheltered place, if possible, although this is not entirely necessary, as the cooking can be done on the open plain in any weather. The advantage of a sheltered place is that it will prevent sand and dirt from getting into the food. In using the cooker, when the food is prepared and in the cooker place, close the same, and cook as in the kitchen. Any water, muddy or salt, can be used in the bottom for the purpose of making steam, only using fresh water for cooking the food. In cooking in summer, when the food is done the fire may be allowed to go out, and if the cooker is kept closed the food will keep warm for two hours, and by this means picket guards and scouting parties coming in late can always have warm food, and while left in the cooker the food will never get dry. In cold weather there should be a small fire kept under the stove. The steamer should never be opened until it is time for the food to be done, giving plenty of time.

FIELD OVENS.

Field ovens for bread baking are of two classes: The first is constructed where the troops are located, by excavations in the earth, or from any material available, such as sod, wood, brush, etc.; these are immovable. The second class have a part or whole of the oven of a portable character, and can be worked with little or no delay or preparation after their arrival in camp.

Dimensions.—The maximum capacity of the hearth of a field oven should be such that at a single baking it does not exceed 150 or 200 rations, unless its arch be of brick or stone

The ration loaf of the United States Army, in pans, should occupy from 25 to 31 square inches. The greater the space the better the bread.

The following table gives the capacities of field ovens with the proportionate dimensions of their hearths:

Capacity of Oven (Number of Rations Single Baking)	Square Inches of Surface to a Ration Loaf	Total Dimensions of the Hearth	Length of Hearth	Width of Hearth
		Square Feet.	*Feet.*	*Feet.*
100	25	17.5	5	3.5
100	30	20.8	5.41+	3.75
150	25	26	6	4.33+
150	30	31.25	6.58+	4.75
200	25	34.58	6.91+	5
200	30	41.25	7.5	5.5

Ovens made of earth, mud, sod, and frames of twigs would be more stable and durable if their capacity did not exceed 100 rations.

AN OVEN IN A STEEP BANK (PLATE 10).

This is recommended as a very good and convenient oven. A bank from 4 to 6 feet high is the best for the purpose. Two men with a spade and a long-handled shovel can build it, in light soil, in three-quarters of an hour. If such tools are not available, it may be constructed with trowel bayonet, intrenching tools, or even with knives. To build the oven, dig down the bank to a vertical face and excavate at the base a hole from 4 to 5 feet horizontally,

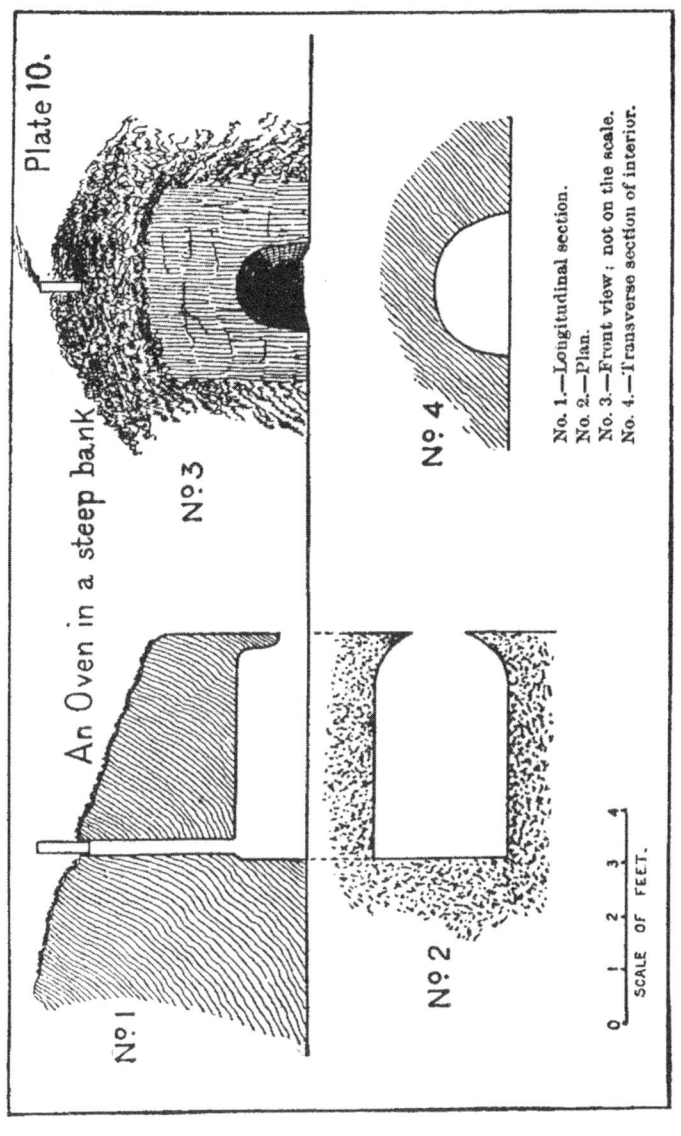

Plate 10.

An Oven in a steep bank

Nº 1
Nº 2
Nº 3
Nº 4

No. 1.—Longitudinal section.
No. 2.—Plan.
No. 3.—Front view; not on the scale.
No. 4.—Transverse section of interior.

SCALE OF FEET.
0 1 2 3 4

care being taken to keep the entrance as small as possible; hollow out the sides of the excavation and arch the roof until the floor is about 2 feet 6 inches in its widest part and the roof 16 inches high in the center of the arch. Then tap the back end for the flue. A hole from 4 to 6 inches in diameter will furnish a good draft. A piece of tent stovepipe may be utilized for this purpose. It will be advantageous, before using, to wet the whole interior surface of the oven and smooth it over neatly, drying it out and hardening it with a small fire. The time required for drying out will depend upon the character of the soil; if ordinarily dry, a fire kept up for an hour will suffice.

Such an oven has a capacity of about 40 rations, and will bake good bread in about 50 minutes. With proper care it will last several weeks. Bake-pans may be used in baking, if they can be obtained; if not, the bare floor, after the ashes are removed, may be used to bake on. After the introduction of the dough, the flue and door should be closed, which may be done with logs of wood, pieces of hard-bread boxes plastered with mud, flat stones, a wet grain sack or piece of canvas. After the oven has been heated, the degree of heat may be regulated by means of the door and flue—opening or closing them as may be necessary.

AN OVEN ON LEVEL GROUND (PLATE 11).

To build such an oven dig a hole about 4 feet long, 1 foot 6 inches deep, and 1 foot 6 inches wide. Without enlarging the top, hollow out the sides, from above downward, until the floor is about 2 feet 6 inches wide. The sides will thus form something of an arch, and be much better than vertical sides. At about one foot from the end dig a trench of convenient dimensions for one man to stand in, to attend to the oven. A suitable size would be 2 feet 6 inches in depth, 4 feet in length, and 2 feet 6 inches in width. Dig down the partition between the oven and the trench for the door. At the back end of the oven dig a small hole, slanting downward, for the flue. Lay green poles close together across the oven, and stop up the interstices with grass or weeds; then plaster over the covering with a thick layer of stiff mud, after which place more poles across and cover with another layer of mud. If pressed for time this last mud may be omitted, and grain sacks or brush may be spread over the second layer of poles and dry earth shoveled on. Dig a ditch around the oven and trench to keep out water in rainy weather.

Such an oven may be built by two men in one hour and a half. It is not durable, as the roof must soon burn out, but it has the advantage of being easily

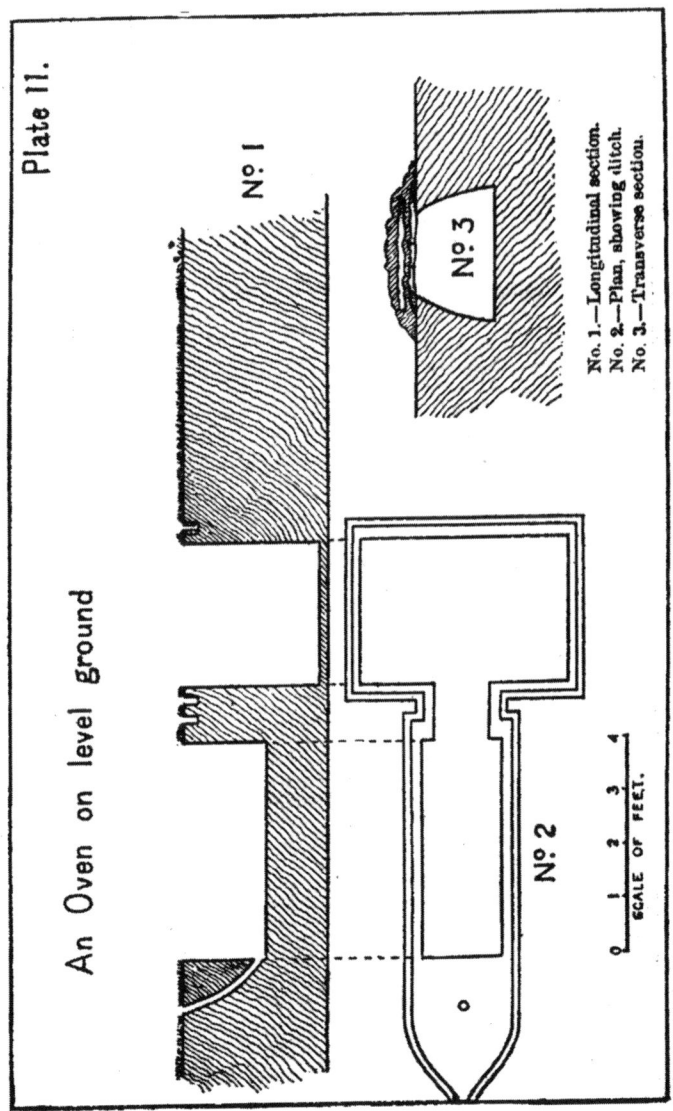

Plate II.

An Oven on level ground

Nº 1

Nº 2

Nº 3

No. 1.—Longitudinal section.
No. 2.—Plan, showing ditch.
No. 3.—Transverse section.

SCALE OF FEET.

0 1 2 3 4

constructed and available for immediate use. Although much inferior to the clay or bank oven, it might sometimes be serviceable to troops on the march.

When there is no bank near, and it is expected to occupy camp for several days, the best plan, perhaps, is to make an artificial bank by digging a pit about 4 feet long, 3 feet wide, and 5 feet deep, and then to build a bank oven. The pit should be protected from rain.

Another method for level ground is to build, over a mound raised for the purpose, a semicylindrical-shaped oven of clay or earth. Any soil suitable for making adobes is good. If lime is available, mortar should be used; if not to be obtained, chopped hay will add strength to the mud.

To build such an oven a rounded heap of dry earth or sand, about 5 feet long, 2 feet 6 inches wide, and 1 foot 9 inches high, should be raised. This is the mold on which the oven is to be formed. Sand is more suitable for the mold than earth, it being more readily removed. Willow twigs bent over and closely wattled together, or a flour barrel laid flat and covered completely with earth, will likewise suffice to give form to the mold. Mix a stiff mud or mortar, and plaster the mold over 5 or 6 inches thick, commencing at the base. Allow one or two days for it to dry and harden, plastering up all cracks which may appear. When nearly dry, cut out the door at one end and the flue at the top of the other end. A small mud chimney raised over the flue will greatly improve the draft. Carefully withdraw the loose earth or sand from the interior. If a barrel has been used for the mold it may be burned out without damaging the oven. Keep a small fire in the oven for at least half a day before attempting to bake. Dig a pit in front of the oven for the convenience of the baker.

Two men can build this oven in three hours, but it will generally not be fit for use for two days. It will last several weeks, and prove very satisfactory. This oven may also be built dome-shaped, like the household ovens used by the Mexicans. This kind of an arch would be stronger than the semicylindrical form, but with the same quantity of material used would not have as great a baking capacity.

The clay oven is peculiarly adapted for use when camping on swampy ground. Under such circumstances it may be constructed upon a platform of stones or logs covered with clay.

DUTCH OVENS.

Considerable fuel is consumed in baking in Dutch ovens where a company is to be supplied—the capacity of each oven being small and several fires being usually required. Fuel may be economized, however, by building the fire in a trench of sufficient length to receive all the ovens.

Care should be taken that the ovens and lids are quite hot before the dough is placed for baking. During the preparations for the baking the ovens and lids should be heated over the fire in the trench. When a good mass of coals has been obtained, the dough should be placed in the heated ovens and the lids put on. The ovens should then be embedded in the coals and the lids covered with coals and hot ashes. If there are not enough coals to cover the lids a small fire may be built over each.

Mess pans may be used in a similar manner for baking bread, but great care will be necessary to prevent burning, owing to the thinness of the metal.

DOUGH.

Dough may be mixed in mess pans, on a piece of canvas, on a rubber blanket, or in the flour barrel or flour sack.

Dough should be set near the fire, and be allowed to rise well before baking. Very little fire is required at first.

If time and fuel are to be considered, biscuits will prove more suitable than large loaves.

FIELD BAKE HOUSES.

During good weather a tent fly, awning, paulin, tent, or interior of a wagon will answer for a temporary shelter under which the labor of the baker can be performed, but in rainy or cold weather a board or more substantial building is essential.

To knead and raise bread successfully in the field with a temperature below 65° or 70° F. requires a long time, and is attended with difficulties and much uncertainty.

UTENSILS NECESSARY FOR A FIELD OVEN.

One dough trough and cover made of pine plank 2 or 2.25 inches thick, about 2 feet 6 inches wide at top and 22 inches at the bottom, and about 18 inches in depth. Length to correspond with capacity of oven. For an oven with capacity of 100 rations, 5 feet long will be sufficient.

Two sets of boards for each trough to separate flour, sponge, and dough.

One board for dough about 4 feet long, 2 feet wide, and 2 inches thick.

One oven peel, wood; blade about 10 inches wide, pole 2 feet longer than
   the oven.
One short-handled brush.
Two large-sized common knives.
Two camp kettles.
One yeast tub (two better).
Two wooden pails, ordinary size, without paint.
A shelter in which to make and keep the bread warm.

BAKING BREAD IN FIELD OVENS.

It not unfrequently occurs that the first baking in a field oven is of a bad
quality; the bread is burnt at the top and not cooked enough at the bottom.
This shows ordinarily that a hearth made on the natural soil is not as dry as the
other parts of the oven, and if you have the time and means it should be paved.

In regard to French field ovens it is stated that the average temperature
for baking is about 250° F., when the bread is placed in, and it is so managed
that when it is baked the temperature has not fallen below 180° F. (This would
appear to be an error, or the loaves should be made very small and thin; even
then a thorough soaking or crusting could not be satisfactorily done.) If not
baked in one hour's time it is permitted to remain in the oven about fifteen
minutes longer, but after this delay it must be taken out, or it will lose more
than gain by remaining.

The best temperature for baking in field ovens is from 380° to 450° F. If
higher, the fermentation, not always perfect in raising the dough, in the open
air, will be stopped too soon. If below this, it will require too long a time to
properly bake.

KNEADING TROUGHS.

An expeditious means of constructing a kneading trough in the field
consists in digging two trenches of unequal size, parallel, *a* and *b*. The first
should be lined with plank; the solid earth which separates the two trenches
should, in the second trench, be sustained by boards also, or pickets at a proper
slope. The bakers descend into the large trench *b* and knead the dough in the
trench *a*, in the trough.

To make sure of the bread rising in the open air, make an excavation about
18 inches deep of convenient length and width. Heat it with pieces of wood in

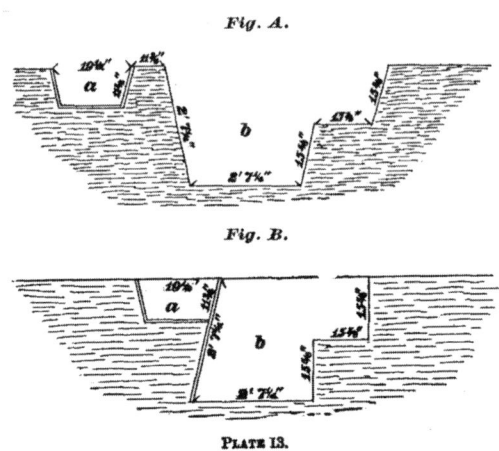

Fig. A.

Fig. B.

PLATE 13.

small sticks, and place the bread on brush-wood, covering the excavation with branches, plank, hay, or grass.

Figs. A and B are two modes of making kneading troughs by excavation and plank. Vertical sections perpendicular to their length.

PORTABLE OVENS.

This class of ovens is generally so constructed that they are ready for use at all times. Those on wheels form part of the train of an army. Many patented varieties were used during the late war, in the field, which gave satisfactory results. Constructed mainly of iron, it is claimed the quality of the bread baked in them is inferior to that made in brick or earthen ovens.

SMALL PORTABLE FIELD OVEN (PLATE 14).

The body of each oven is made of two pieces of 1/16 inch sheet iron. These sheets are 5 feet long by 2 feet 6 inches wide, and so curved that, when their upper edges are connected and the lower edges fixed in the ground, they form an arch, the span of which is 3 feet 9 inches and the rise 1 foot 4 inches. The lower edge of each sheet is bent outward into a flange, so as to secure a firm rest on the ground.

On the inside of each sheet are riveted 3 longitudinal bars, 1 inch wide and ⅜ inch thick, and on the outside 5 transverse ribs, 1¼ inches wide by ⅜ inch thick (fig. 2). The upper ends of the transverse ribs on one of the sheets are formed into hooks, and those of the other sheet into eyes, by means of which the sheets are securely attached to each other along the ridge of the oven when erected.

The front of the oven is closed by a two-handled iron door (fig. 1), which is kept in place by means of hooks and eyes.

When the soil is of clay, or of other favorable quality, the rear end of the oven may be closed by the natural earth; but if it is sandy or loose, a sheet-iron plate will be required to close it. No chimney is necessary.

When set up, the whole, excepting the door, is covered with a mass of earth 8 inches in thickness.

This depth of earth is named for the reason that a larger quantity would be liable, from its weight, to bend the iron when heated, and a smaller quantity would allow too much heat to escape.

An excavation 3 or 4 feet in depth should be made a foot or two from the door, for the convenience of the baker.

Two hours are required for heating the oven at first starting, but for each heating immediately following one hour will be sufficient.

A small quantity of wood is placed in the oven at the extreme rear and ignited, the door being kept open to afford a draft and a vent for the smoke. Small quantities of wood should then be added as combustion progresses. In this way the fuel will burn more freely, and the oven be heated quicker, than if all the fuel necessary for the heating were put in at once.

As soon as the oven is at a white heat the ashes should be raked out, the floor swept clean, and the dough in pans introduced. The door should then be closed, and all interstices filled with moistened clay or earth. Bake pans may be dispensed with if the floor is made of bricks. If bread pans are used they should be of such size that four of them, or at most six, will cover the whole available space of the oven floor. The time required for each baking is about 45 minutes.

As each of the two principal pieces forming an oven weighs only about 85 pounds, the whole—consisting of the two sides, the door, and end plate—can be easily transported, and can even be carried on a pack animal if necessary.

To set up the oven no tools except a pickax and a shovel are required, the sides being merely placed on level ground, attached together, the rear end closed, and the whole covered with earth. It can be erected and prepared for use in 15 minutes, and if kept in constant operation for 24 hours can bake

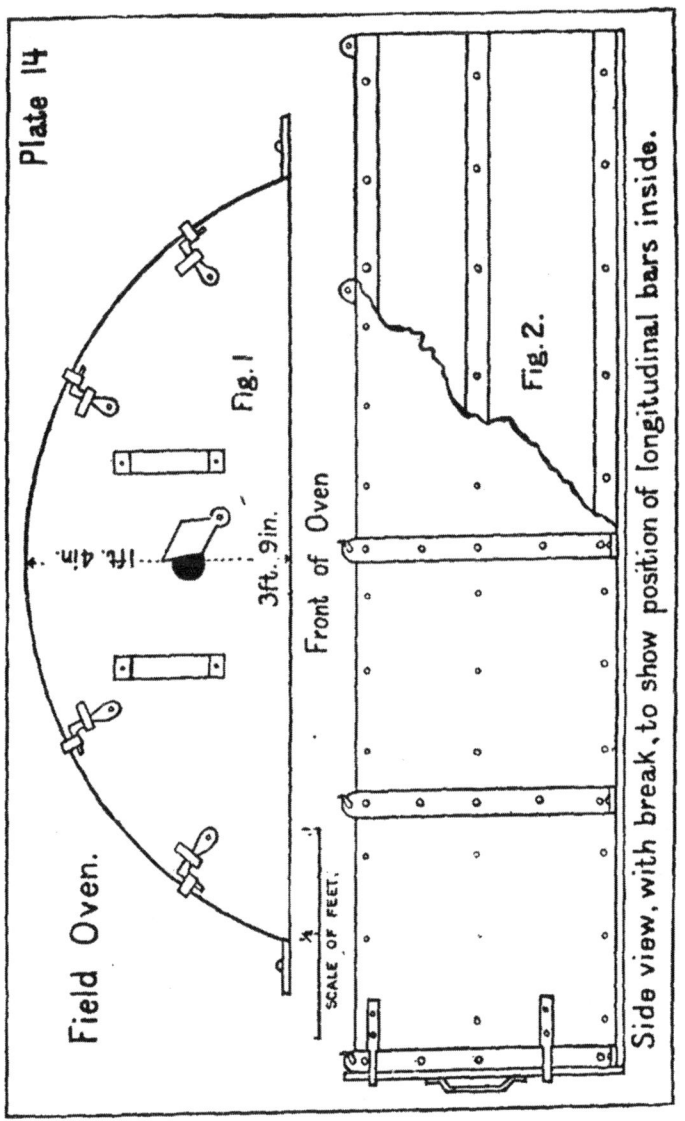

Plate 14

Field Oven.

Fig. 1

Front of Oven

1ft. 4in.

3ft. 9in.

SCALE OF FEET.

Fig. 2.

Side view, with break, to show position of longitudinal bars inside.

sufficient bread for 1,000 men. By the use of two of these ovens, therefore, a regiment of a thousand men, if it make a halt of 14 hours each day, can be supplied with fresh bread daily on the line of march.

The dough is kneaded in the field by hand, and the operation requires about 45 minutes. Ordinary kneading troughs for the purpose are made, which may be placed on trestles, or they may be fixed on the ground and trenches excavated near them for the kneaders to stand in.

PORTABLE FIELD OVEN OF A LARGER SIZE

The body (top and sides) of this oven is made in two parts, each part being in shape nearly the quarter of a cylinder, and formed of three pieces of sheet iron 3 feet long by 2 feet 2 inches wide and $\frac{3}{16}$ inch thick, riveted together, and overlapping 2 inches (fig. 2).

Each side has three transverse bars of iron, $1\frac{1}{2}$ inches wide and $\frac{3}{8}$ inch thick, riveted on the outside. The upper ends of the bars on one of the sides are formed into hooks, and those of the other side into eyes, by means of which the two parts are connected and held firmly together along the ridge of the oven when erected.

The lower edge of each side for a width of 3 inches along its entire length is bent outward into a flange, the lower face of which coincides with the plane of the bed of the oven.

A longitudinal strip of light sheet iron, $2\frac{1}{2}$ inches wide, is riveted along the upper edge of the side on which the eyes are, and the edge of the other side slips under it in hooking (fig. 4).

To each side, on the under front end of the oven, are riveted two short iron bars, $5\frac{1}{2}$ inches long, $1\frac{1}{2}$ inches wide, and $\frac{3}{16}$ inch thick, each with a small hole in the outer end, and which are so bent as to pass through slots in the face of the front of the oven, and are caught outside by corresponding hooks, as shown in the drawing (fig. 3).

COOKING AND MESS FURNITURE FOR FIELD SERVICE.

The device for cooking, as now furnished by the Ordnance Department, is one meat can and plate combined, and consists of two oval dishes made of block tin, one deeper than the other, which fit together, forming a meat-ration can of the following dimensions:

Length, 8 inches; width, $6\frac{1}{2}$ inches; depth of whole can, $1\frac{1}{2}$ inches when closed; the lower dish to be 1 inch in depth; the plate $\frac{3}{4}$ inch in depth.

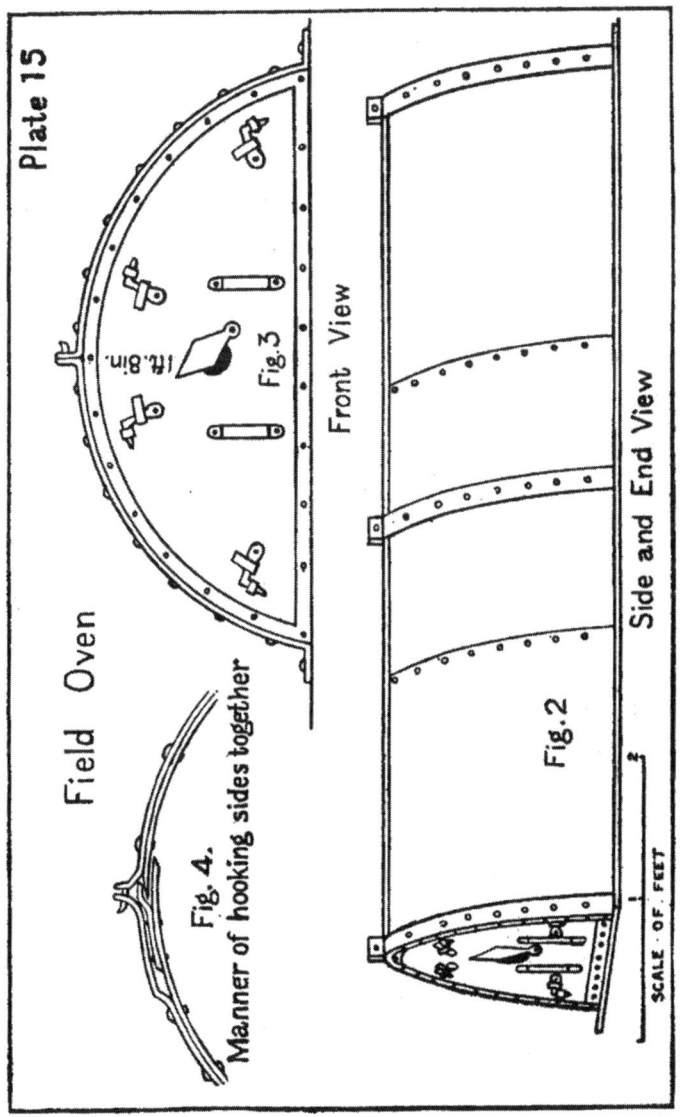

Plate 15

Field Oven

Fig. 4.
Manner of hooking sides together

Fig. 3

Front View

Fig. 2

Side and End View

SCALE · OF · FEET

1ft. 8in.

To the deeper dish or plate is attached a light iron handle, which folds over and holds the two together. The one with the handle may be used to eat soup out of; as a frying pan; or to warm up cold food, and many other purposes that will suggest themselves when it is used.

These articles are, on the march, placed in the haversack (the cup being attached to the strap), which also contains the rations required to be carried by the soldier and, with the canteen, which holds three pints, constitute the cooking and eating utensils that are deemed essential for use upon the most active service.

COOKING AND MESS FURNITURE FOR FIELD SERVICE (PLATE 16).

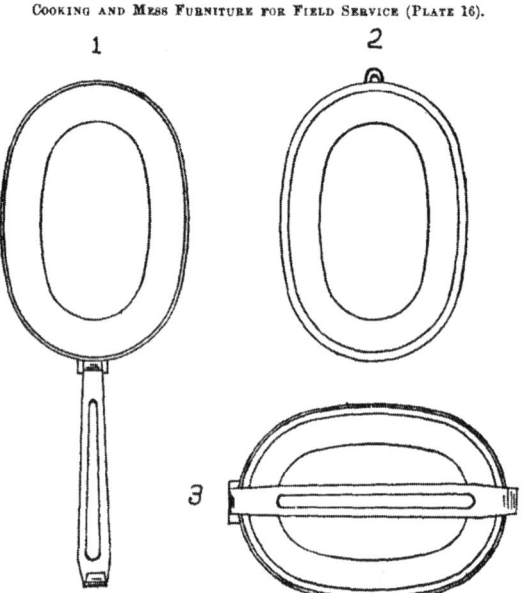

1 Soup plate   2 Plate.
    3 Meat Can, Closed.

HINTS REGARDING WATER AND WOOD.

Nothing is more certain to secure endurance and capability of long-continued effort than the avoidance of everything as a drink except cold water (and coffee at breakfast). Drink as little as possible of even cold water. Experience teaches old soldiers that the less they drink on a march the better, and that they suffer less in the end by controlling the desire to drink, however urgent.

After any sort of exhausting effort a cup of coffee or tea, hot or cold, is an admirable sustainer of the strength until nature begins to recover herself.

Officers in command of companies should impress upon their men the danger to which they expose themselves in drinking bad water. Poisonous matter of many descriptions may be taken into the stomach in it. (In Algeria, leeches have in this manner been frequently taken into the body, causing dangerous internal bleeding.) Dysentery and diarrhea ensue and, in the opinion of the best army surgeons, it is one of the chief causes of those fearful diseases which have devastated armies in so many wars. It has lately been proved, that if bad water does not produce cholera, its use predisposes the body to take it when it is prevalent.

TO PURIFY WATER THAT IS MUDDY, PUTRID, OR SALT.

With muddy water, the remedy is to filter; with putrid, to boil, to mix with charcoal, or expose to the sun and air; or, what is best, to use all three methods at the same time. With salt water nothing avails but distillation.

TO FILTER MUDDY WATER.

When at the watering place there is nothing but wet sand, take a good handful of grass and tie it roughly together in the form of a cone, six or eight inches long; then dipping the broad end into the puddle and turning it up, a streamlet of partly-filtered water will trickle down through the small end. For a copious supply the most perfect plan, if you have means, is to bore a cask full of auger holes and put another small one, that has had the bottom knocked out, inside it; then fill up the space between the two with grass, moss, etc. Now, sinking the whole in the midst of the pond, the water will filter through the auger holes and moss and rise up clear of, at least, weeds and sand in the inner cask, whence it can be ladled. With a single cask, the lower part of the sides may be bored and alternate layers of sand and grass thrown in till they reach above the holes; through these layers the water will strain. Or any coarse bag that is kept open with hoops, made on the spot, may be moored in the muddy pool by having a heavy stone put inside of it, and will act on the same principle, but less efficiently than the casks. Sand, charcoal, sponge, and wool are the substances most commonly used in filters; peat charcoal is excellent. A small piece of alum is very efficacious in purifying water from organic matter, which is precipitated by the alum and a deposit left at the bottom of the vessel.

PUTRID WATER

should always be boiled with charcoal or charred sticks before drinking, as low fevers and dysenteries too often are the consequence of its being used indiscreetly, but the charcoal entirely disinfects it; bitter herbs, if steeped in it, or even rubbed well about the cup, are said to render it less unwholesome. The Indians plunge a hot iron into putrid and muddy water.

When carrying water in buckets, put a wreath of grass, or something floating on the top of the water, to prevent splashing; and also make a hoop, inside which the porter walks, while his laden hands rest on the rim, the office of the hoop being to keep the buckets from knocking against his legs.

TO CLARIFY MUDDY WATER.

Sprinkle a pinch of pulverized alum over the water in the bucket, and the impurities will soon settle at the bottom.

TO KINDLE A SPARK INTO A FLAME,

the spark should be received into a kind of loose nest of the most inflammable substances at hand, which ought to be prepared before the tinder is lighted. When by careful blowing or fanning the flame is once started, it should be fed with little bits of sticks or bark, split with a knife or rubbed between the fingers into fibers, until it has gained enough strength to grapple with thicker ones.

FUEL.

There is something of a knack in finding firewood. It should be looked for under bushes. The stump of a tree, that is rooted nearly to the ground, has often a magnificent root, fit to blaze throughout the night. Dry manure of cattle is an excellent fuel. Dry fuel gives out far more heat than damp fuel. Bones of animals also furnish an excellent substitute for firewood.

FIREWOOD

should be cut into lengths of 1 foot and about 2 inches square. When nothing but brushwood is to be had, the trench should be deepened where the fire is lit. Damp or very sappy wood should be avoided. Bones can be used when other fuel is not to be had. During a march, it is well to pick up and throw into the wagons all the dry wood that may be found along the road.

FILTERS.

Two barrels, one inside the other, having a space of 4 or even 6 inches clear all around between them filled with layers of sand, gravel, and charcoal, form an excellent filter. The inside one, without a bottom, rests on stones embedded in sand, the sand reaching above the chine, and above this, between the barrels, is a layer of charcoal and of coarse gravel.

The water, flowing or being poured into the space between the two, and having thus to force its way through these substances into the inner barrel, becomes purified. The water is drawn off by means of a pipe running through the outer into the inner barrel.

SUGGESTIONS RELATIVE TO COOKS AND THEIR DU-TIES.

There should be required for each organization of 60 men one chief cook, one assistant cook, and one man detailed daily as cook's police. While the chief cook may be confronted by conditions entirely different from those to which he is accustomed in garrison, he will get willing assistance from other members of the company, and thus have more time for general supervision.

With the exception of the first sergeant there is no non-commissioned officer in the company so important to its well being as a competent, energetic chief cook.

His particular duties comprise (1) cooking, and baking bread, (2) care of rations, and (3) general superintendence of all work in the kitchen, and responsibility for all rations and cooking furniture. If there is a good baker in the company it might sometimes be found well to give him charge (under the chief cook) of all the bread baking.

The assistant cook assists the chief cook in his various duties, and is held responsible for the cleanliness of the cooking utensils.

The cook's police assists the cooks as directed—the cutting of wood and keeping up of fires usually being included in his duties.

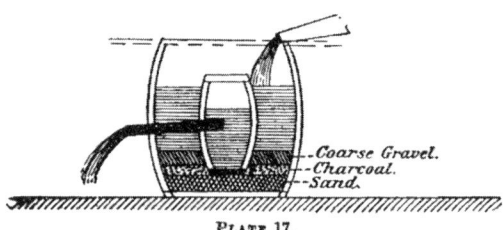

.Coarse Gravel.
.Charcoal.
.Sand.

PLATE 17.

In the cavalry it is usual to allow the cooks to ride with the wagons or pack train. When both wagons and packs are provided, the cooks ride with the latter, and should always have on the pack mules sufficient rations and utensils with which to prepare a meal upon arrival in camp.

SECURING AND TRANSPORTING RATIONS.

For use in garrison, as well as in the field, each company should be provided with facilities for carrying the ration. It will be found convenient to have a ration box of outside dimensions which will just admit of its being placed in the rear end of an army wagon, which is about 40 inches wide. The following is a description of a ration box which has been found by actual service to answer all requirements (see plate 18):

Its outside dimensions over all are 38½ by 38½ by 30 inches deep. It is made of white pine 1 inch thick and doubled or re-enforced for 3 inches at top and bottom; the edges should be dovetailed, the corners strengthened with angle iron and braces, and the sides provided with suitable handles. The interior, as shown in plan, is divided by vertical partitions, which extend to within 8 inches of the top. Exactly flush with the tops of these partitions, and extending around the interior of the larger compartment, are strips a, b, c, which support a square false lid of good 1-inch hard wood a little smaller than the inside dimensions of the box, and in the edges of which hand-holes are cut as shown in plan. This false lid may be used as a bread board, a chopping board, and for a variety of other purposes.

The real top or lid is secured by three strong hinges, and provided with suitable lock and key. .

The space between the real and false lids is used for carrying fresh bread for the first camp, and smaller utensils, dishcloths, etc.

Such a box will weigh about 180 pounds, and will hold, in ration sacks to be described later, 1,000 rations each of sugar, coffee, salt, soap, and pepper; 200 rations of beans, a 10-pound can of lard, and 25 pounds of flour—the latter to be used in making gravies.

For field use, ration sacks of strong drilling or ticking with permanent ties, should also be provided.

Each ration sack should be marked in solid black indelible letters with the name of the article which it is to hold, and should ordinarily be large enough to contain 10 days' supply for the company of the component of the ration to be carried therein.

As soon as an original package is opened the contents should be transferred to its particular sack.

When wagon transportation is used, these sacks with their contents can be placed in their appropriate compartments in the ration box. When packs are used, an additional covering of gunny sack will be required.

When ordered for field service, and rations have been drawn, the first care must be to pack everything with the greatest possible care. Each side of bacon or piece of meat should be wrapped in several sacks. Coffee, sugar, salt, beans, rice, etc., except that which is carried in the ration box, should be double sacked.

Matches should be kept in closed tin boxes, or in wide-mouth bottles, and well corked, so that no dampness can reach them.

Candles should be wrapped up and placed in a candle box, or in a compartment of the mess box, to prevent their being broken.

Cases containing pepper and yeast powder should be opened and the contents carefully repacked with hay or straw, so as to prevent the cans from being shaken open and their contents spilled. Flour and vegetables should be double sacked and sacks securely sewed or tied. Boxes of hard bread require no special attention.

One full day's ration of soft bread and fresh meat should be drawn for the first day's march; also a proportion of one-fifth or more of hard bread, to meet the contingencies of wet weather or lack of fuel for baking purposes.

If the company be supplied with a Buzzacott oven, about all the utensils necessary for the mess will be found with the oven; otherwise, the following (all to be ascertained by inspection to be in serviceable condition) should be taken, if possible:

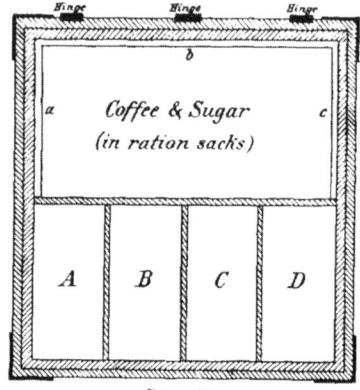

PLATE 13.

PLAN OF RATION BOX.

Scale $\frac{1}{8}$.

a, *b*, *c*, cleats for supporting false lid, the upper edges of which are on same level as tops of partitions.

A, *B*, *C*, *D*, compartments for beans, rice, candles, soap, salt, and ground coffee, all in ration sacks. Yeast powder and pepper in cans and carefully packed. Coffee mill, etc.

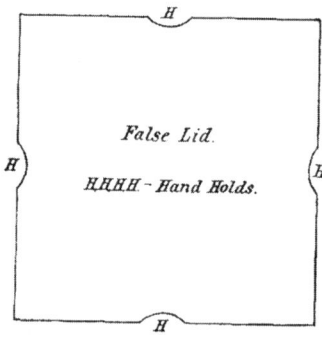

Four frying pans.

Six camp kettles (two sets or "nests").

Twenty mess pans (ten deep and ten shallow).

Three butcher knives.

One steel.

Two long-handled spoons.

Two long-handled forks.

Two dippers.

One skimmer.

One small coffee mill, and coffee roaster. (Plate No. 19.)

One iron kettle rod, twelve feet long and one inch in diameter, and supplied with six or more kettle hooks.

Two iron uprights, one inch in diameter and four feet long.

One spring balance (one which will weigh up to 200 pounds is to be preferred, as being useful when purchases of fresh beef, forage, etc., are made).

Two axes and one camp hatchet.

The smaller articles can be placed in a small wooden box fastened about with a strap, while the knives may he carried in leather sheaths attached to the cartridge belts of the cooks.

In packing the wagons the tents, bedding rolls, etc., should be put in first and a space left at the tail end of the wagon for the mess box and cooking outfit. If the wagon be crowded, the Buzzacott oven can be lashed to the rear of the wagon outside the tail gate, the side resting in the feed box.

The chief cook should know where everything is when wagons are packed, to save time in searching for articles should anything be wanted during a temporary halt. All articles necessary for the first meal should be so placed in the wagons that they can be taken out at once, and no delay occur in the preparation of the meal.

Before leaving a post the chief cook should roast a part of his coffee, so that if unexpectedly called upon to make coffee he will not find himself unprepared. Roasted coffee should always be kept on hand.

When pack transportation is provided each troop should have four mess boxes, $\frac{7}{8}$-inch lumber, dovetailed, 11 by 18 by 26 inches, and when packed in pack cover, without lids.

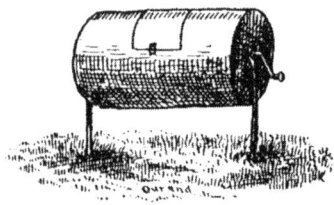

PLATE 19.

The rations should be carefully put up in 100-pound packs lashed solidly, and carried on the best pack mules; each pack is plainly marked with its contents and weighed.

Salt, sugar, coffee, and beans are double sacked and lashed in 100-pound packages. Bacon in 100-pound packages, is packed in from 5 to 8 pounds of clean straw or hay, double sacked, and lashed firmly.

Each cargo is in two side packs of about 100 to 125 pounds each, and should match in size, shape, and weight, as nearly as practicable; each side pack having, as nearly as may be, the following proportions: width, one-half more than the thickness; length nearly one-half more than width—e. g., 12 by 18 by 25 inches.

The salt, sugar, coffee, and beans should not all be placed in one cargo.

When no transportation is provided, which may occur in maneuver marches in the presence of the enemy, troops may be required to carry their rations on the person. It may safely be said, in general terms, that a soldier can carry three days' subsistence on his person—the infantryman in the haversack or pack, the cavalryman in his saddlebags. Under such conditions of course only bacon (one day's ration of which may be replaced by cooked beef), hard bread, coffee, sugar, salt, and pepper can be carried, the other components being replaced by such condensed forms of food as compressed soup, etc.

The regulation meat can, tin cup, knife, fork and spoon answer all requirements for cooking under such emergencies.

CAMPING.

Upon arrival in camp as soon as ranks are broken in the infantry, or the horses provided for in the cavalry, the first sergeant commands: "All hands out for wood and water," when all available men prepare to gather fuel and carry water to the spot selected for the kitchen. If the transportation has arrived in camp, the cooks, while waiting the arrival of fuel and water, proceed to unload the articles necessary for a meal; the assistant cook and cook's police dig a shallow trench about 10 feet long, 18 inches deep, and 12 inches wide. The kettle rod is placed in position over this trench, the fire lighted, and the kettles with their contents hung on the hooks, as quickly as possible, and the meal prepared while tents are being put up. As a rule, a meal should be served about 30 minutes after the transportation reaches camp. This meal should, therefore, be of a simple character, such as bacon, bread, and coffee; the more elaborate meal to follow later in the day or evening. Immediately after the meal has been served, the chief cook proceeds to prepare the articles necessary for the next meal, and the assistant cook to cleaning and scouring the utensils. While they are thus employed, the police should dig another shallow trench at right angles to and connecting with the first trench. In this a small fire should be started to thoroughly dry the ground.

The fire for baking may then be easily gotten from the cook fire. The cook having made everything ready for the next meal, may then turn the care of them to the assistant and proceed to bake his bread for the next day.

The dough may be mixed on a rubber blanket or false cover of the ration box, according to the formula printed on the yeast-powder can, each particular brand of powder needing a different proportion; and may then be baked in the Buzzacott oven or mess pans. If mess pans are to be used, the dough is then placed in the deeper pans and covered with the shallow ones. An even bed of coals is then raked into the baking trench, the ovens or pans placed on this bed and live coals placed on top. Care should be taken not to use too many coals, as owing to the thinness of the pans, the contents are easily burned.

After the evening meal, which should usually be immediately after retreat, the necessary articles are prepared for breakfast, and everything that can possibly be spared is repacked into the wagons, so that there may be no delay in the morning, or confusion if obliged to start during the night. In making his calculation for breakfast, he should be careful not to overestimate, as he will find it difficult to carry the remnants from one camp to another, and consequently a loss may occur.

The cook fire is replenished during the night by members of the guard, care being taken to use as little fuel as possible.

The cooks are awakened usually about two hours before reveille, so that breakfast may be served immediately after that formation.

If this be done there will be ample time between breakfast and the "general" for the cooks to have everything used at breakfast cleaned up and in readiness to be loaded into the wagon. If breakfast is delayed, pans and kettles can be thrown into the wagon dirty, and warm water will be readily available at the next camp to clean them.

A few close-fitting covers for the camp kettles will prove invaluable, as by their use many articles of food, such as soup stock, etc., may be carried from one camp to another, which would otherwise be thrown away. Beans in soak previous to baking may also be carried in this manner. If possible, all the dry sticks of wood should be placed on the wagon; a fire can then be started immediately upon arrival in camp, without waiting for the arrival of the camp supplies. In like manner, especially in traveling through a poorly-watered country, the water kegs should be filled before leaving camp.

Water kegs should always be filled before leaving camp, even if it is expected to find better water during the march; because, if obliged to camp before reaching water, there will be no lack of that necessary article. Upon reaching the watering place, the kegs can always be emptied and refilled.

TEMPORARY CAMPS.

The internal economy of the company kitchen in temporary camp differs but little from that which obtains on the march, except in the following:

A brush wind-break six or eight feet high should be erected on the windward side of the fire.

This prevents in a great measure sand and dirt from being blown into the food, and the inclosure forms a capital kitchen.

Rations should be taken from the wagons, if to be in camp for two days or more, and thoroughly overhauled, piled up neatly and covered with a paulin or wagon sheet; everything being disposed of, however, in such a way that the wagons may be packed on short notice if the command is unexpectedly ordered to march.

There being more opportunity for the preparation of soups, stews, etc., than when on the march, they should be made more frequently. In camp, whenever practicable, the bacon and any other components on which a saving can be made, should be exchanged for fresh meats and vegetables.

RECIPES FOR CAMP COOKERY.

MISCELLANEOUS HINTS.

Bread and soup are the great items of a soldier's diet in every situation; to make them well is an essential part of his instruction. Those great scourges of camp—scurvy and diarrhea—more frequently result from want of skill in cooking than from any other cause whatever. Officers in command, and, more immediately regimental officers, should therefore give strict attention to this vital branch of interior economy.

Men should never eat heartily just before a great undertaking, because the nervous power is irresistibly drawn to the stomach to manage the food eaten, thus draining off that supply which the brain and muscles so much need.

It is always best to prepare hot meals when possible. If preserved or cooked rations have been served out, and there is time, they should be warmed or made into soup or *bouilli* before being eaten.

Fresh meat ought not to be cooked before it has had time to bleed and cool; and meats should generally be boiled, with a view to soup; though sometimes roasted or baked, for variety.

Fresh meat issued to the soldiers in advance, in hot weather, may be preserved by half boiling it; or, if there be not time for that operation, the meat may be kept some twenty-four hours, by previously exposing it for a few minutes to a very thick smoke.

Salted meats should soak eight or ten hours, or the water they are boiled in should be changed several times.

Vinegar added to water that tough meats are boiled in, tends to make them tender.

Meats to be eaten cold should be placed in boiling water. This sets the juices; while meat put first in cold water and then gradually heated and boiled, has its juices extracted; best done this way in soups, stews, etc.

Vegetables, especially fresh ones, should be immersed in boiling water; dried vegetables in cold water.

Meats that are to be used cold, ham especially, should be allowed to cool in the liquid in which they were boiled, as they will then be especially sweet, juicy and tender.

SOUP.

Hang the camp kettle on the crane, and use a cover to keep out ashes, sand, or dust. If any fresh lean meat is available, put in a small piece, after cutting off every particle of fat. After breakfast build a fire of logs under the camp kettle, and let the meat boil in an abundance of water for two hours or longer, or until the meat is almost ready to drop to pieces; then add Irish potatoes and onions, all cut up, and simmer until the vegetables are done. While boiling, frequently skim from the top every particle of grease that rises. When done, season with pepper and salt to taste, and eat hot. If it is not thick enough, mix enough flour and water in a tin cup to the consistency of molasses, and pour slowly into the soup, stirring with a spoon as poured. Good soup may be made with bones, cracked with a hatchet and boiled for a long time, or with vegetables alone, thickened and seasoned. Canned tomatoes make a nice soup.

PEA SOUP, WITH SALT PORK OR BEEF.

(Sufficient for 22 men.)

Meat.	Flour or broken biscuits.
Mixed vegetables.	Pepper.
Split peas.	Water.

Peel, clean, and cut up the vegetables; place the fresh cold water in the camp kettle; add the vegetables and peas, and boil gently until the peas are soft. Then put into the soup about two pounds of meat, which should have been previously well washed in cold water, and simmer gently till it is cooked; then take it out and cover it up to keep warm.

Mix some flour into a smooth batter with cold water, and add it to the soup, keeping it well stirred to prevent it burning; boil for thirty minutes and serve. If flour is not to be had, use instead powdered biscuits, previously soaked in cold water.

The remainder of the meat should be soaked and well washed in cold water, then put into the camp kettle, with sufficient water to cover it, and allowed to boil for thirty minutes; the water in which it was boiled should now be thrown away, the camp kettle refilled with fresh cold water, and the meat boiled till done.

BOILED SOUP DUMPLING.

Make a light dough, or procure from the bakery, dough which is ready for the oven.

Flour the hands well and mold the dough into balls about the size of an egg. Drop them successively into boiling water. Boil in the soup about fifteen minutes.

STEWS OF BEEF OR MUTTON.

Joint or cut up your meat in small pieces, and place in the stewpan; add a couple of slices of bacon, cut thin; a few raw onions, peeled and cut up; pepper and salt to taste.

Pour in hot water until you have covered the meat with about two inches of water on top; put the lid on and simmer slowly until the water has boiled down, say one-half, or until it becomes thick or milky from the juices extracted from the meats. If it is too thin to be palatable, thicken with grated hard bread, or a paste of water and flour, mixed in a tin cup and poured into the stew.

IRISH STEW, WITH SALT BEEF.

Meat.	Potatoes.
Onions.	Pepper.

Wash and clean the meat in cold water; separate it from the bone, and cut it into small pieces of about two ounces each, and wash it well again in cold water; peel and clean the potatoes, peel and slice the onions; place the meat, potatoes, and onions in the camp kettle, add a little pepper and sufficient cold water to cover the whole; put the lid on the kettle and cook gently over a slow fire, frequently skimming the fat off the top.

A GOOD STEW.

Use meats, game especially, of any or various kinds—prairie chicken, quail, duck, rabbit, turkey—or if you have no fresh meats or game, use fried bacon or pork.

Into a kettle put a layer of bacon, meats, etc., and season; dredge with flour, then add a layer of potatoes, onions, etc.; repeating this until the kettle is nearly full, as desired. Over all pour sufficient broth or water (the former preferable) to cover, and stew slowly from one to three hours, according to size. During the last hour stir in a quart of batter to thicken; season to taste and serve hot.

HOT MEAT STEW, WITH GARNISH.

Take cold meats, game especially, cut up into pieces of small and equal size; put them into the largest pan with broth or cold water, a few quarts of onions, can of tomatoes, etc., and stir slowly for one to two hours, seasoning to taste; then to the quart of flour add six tablespoonfuls of mustard or curry powder, stir in; boil ten minutes more and serve. Use as a garnish either rice, boiled or mashed potatoes, corn, etc.

This is a good hot winter dish.

STEW, WITH CANNED MEATS.

| Meat. | Onions. | Salt. |
| Potatoes. | Pepper. | Water. |

Peel and slice the potatoes and onions; put them in the camp kettle, season with pepper and salt, pour in sufficient water to cover them, and stew gently, keeping the lid of the kettle closely shut until the potatoes are nearly cooked; then open the tins of meat and cut up the contents and put them in the kettle with the potatoes; let the whole simmer for ten minutes, then serve.

BROWN STEW, WITH CANNED MEATS.

| Meat. | Flour. | Salt. |
| Onions. | Pepper. | Water. |

Peel and slice the onions, melt the fat of the meat in the camp kettle, add the onions and fry them until brown, mix the flour into a smooth batter with cold water, season with pepper and salt, and pour it into the camp kettle; stir the whole well together; cut the meat into slices, put it into the kettle, and, when warmed through, serve.

TO ROAST MEATS IN A DUTCH OVEN.

Put about one inch of water in oven, and season with salt and pepper, so as to have a gravy for basting the meat while cooking, thus preventing its becoming too dry. Make a mop by tying a clean rag to the end of a stick; remove the lid frequently, and baste the roast with the gravy. When done remove the meat to a dish; put into the gravy a pinch of flour to thicken, and pour over the roast. If your roast is thick or tough, parboil in camp kettle from thirty minutes to an hour before placing in the oven; then roast to a nice brown.

BROILING STEAKS OR CHOPS.

Build a good log fire, and let it burn down to a bed of coals, so that there will be no smoke. Cut your steak or chops almost one inch thick and season with pepper and salt. Put your meat between the bars of your broiler, and place on the red-hot coals. Broil quickly until rare, or well done, as you desire, frequently turning the broiler from one side to the other, so that the meat will not have time to char.

If a little charred, scrape with a knife; place on hot dish, season with salt and pepper, and serve while hot.

BAKED BEEF HEAD.
(Without cooking utensils.)

Dig in the ground a hole of sufficient size and build a fire in it. After the fuel has burned to coals put in the head, neck downward. Cover it with green grass, coals, and earth. Build a good fire over the buried head and keep it burning for about six hours.

Unearth the head and remove the skin. A head treated in this way at night will be found cooked in the morning. The head of any animal may be cooked in this way.

SALT BEEF AND DUMPLINGS.

Meat.   Flour.   Suet.

Soak and well wash the meat in cold water, and place it in the camp kettle, with plenty of water, and boil gently for one hour; then throw away the water in which it was boiled, and replace it with fresh cold water, and boil till the meat is cooked. Chop the suet up fine, mix it with the flour, and pour in some cold water and well mix the whole, and form it into dumplings about two inches in diameter; place the dumplings in a kettle with the beef about thirty minutes before the latter is cooked, and let both boil together until done.

SALT PORK AND HARD BREAD.

Meat.	Hard bread.
Onions.	Parsley.
Pepper.	Water.

(a) Soak the hard bread in cold water for one hour; wash, clean, and boil the pork; drain the water off the hard bread, and cut up the pork into thin slices; peel and slice the onions, wash and chop up the parsley; pour a little water into the camp kettle; place a layer of the soaked hard bread on top, then another layer of pork, and so on alternately, until the kettle is nearly full. Cover the whole with water, and cook gently over a slow fire for one hour and fifteen minutes, and serve.

(b) Treat the pork, onions, parsley, as in (a); soak the hard bread for two hours, then squeeze it dry; mince up the pork and mix it with the hard bread, onions, parsley and pepper; then roll it into balls, and place them in a camp kettle with sufficient water to cover, and cook gently over a slow fire for one hour, and serve.

These recipes can also be prepared in the camp kettle lids, by placing the layers of pork and hard bread or balls in one camp kettle lid, and covering it with another, and placing a few live embers underneath and on the top of the lids.

TO COOK FISH WITHOUT COOKING UTENSILS.

Dig a hole in the ground about eighteen inches deep, and of sufficient size to contain the fish; build a fire in it and let it burn to coals. Remove the coals, leaving the hot ashes at the bottom, upon which place a thick layer of green grass; place the fish on top and cover with another layer of grass; then rake back the live coals and loose earth and build a small fire on top. At the end of about three-quarters of an hour the fish will be found cooked with the juice retained; the skin will peel off and leave the flesh clean and free from ashes and dirt.

BAKED FISH

should be dressed and cooked whole. Make a stuffing of bread crumbs, pork, onions, etc.; fill the body with same and close with a skewer. Put a little water in the pan; dredge the fish well, season; put a few slices of bacon fat on top and bake from forty-five minutes to an hour. Fish from six to eight pounds are best for baking, or a number of them together.

PLANKED SHAD.

This is the very best way of cooking shad: The plank should be three inches thick, two feet long, one and a half feet wide and of well seasoned hickory or oak. Take a fine shad just from the water, scale, split it down the back, clean it, wash it well and immediately wipe dry. Dredge it with salt and pepper. Place the plank before a clear fire to get very hot. Then spread the shad open and nail it, skin side next to the hot plank, with four large-headed tacks. Put it before the fire, with large end down. In a few minutes turn the board so the other end will be down, and do this every few minutes until the fish is done. To tell when it is done pierce with a fork; if the flesh be flaky it is done. Spread with dripping and serve on the plank, or draw the tacks out carefully and slide the shad onto a hot dish. The whitefish caught in the lakes are excellent when cooked in this manner.

TO BOIL POTATOES WITH THEIR JACKETS ON.

After washing, place in camp kettle and pour on boiling water. Boil slowly until a fork will pierce them with ease. Serve thus, or peel while hot; mash into a paste, season with pepper and salt, and eat hot.

STEWED POTATOES.

Peel and cut into thick slices, stew in stewpan, with enough water to cover them, and add two thin slices of bacon; put on the lid and cook until potatoes are soft and nearly dry, but stir frequently to prevent burning or sticking to the bottom of pan. Add salt and pepper. A raw onion or two cut into the stewing potatoes gives a flavor that a hungry soldier always enjoys.

BAKED BEANS, NO. 1.

Soak the beans over night, if possible, and boil with a piece of pork or bacon about two hours, or until a bean will mash easily between the fingers; then strain them into a pan (pots are the best) and cover them with the liquid boiled in; season well, adding a cupful of molasses or sugar. If pork is salty, more salt will not be required. Draw a knife blade crosswise through the rind of three or four pieces of bacon or pork; bury them in the beans and bake slowly two to three hours or more. Brown the top before serving, but do not let the bottom get dry. Add more liquid as it becomes dry, and do not have too great a heat on bottom; stir from bottom if necessary. Some add vinegar, molasses, and mustard; a small quantity mixed with the beans increases the flavor. If water is hard, a small quantity of saleratus [sodium bicarbonate] when the beans are boiling will soften it.

BAKED BEANS, NO. 2.

Boil the beans for a long time over a brisk fire, until they are perfectly soft, and settle at the bottom of the stewpan. Pour off the water, and let them dry in the stewpan by placing it on hot ashes or coals for a few minutes. When perfectly dry, mash into a fine paste; season with pepper and salt, and place in a conical or round shape on a tin plate.

Lay two thin slices of bacon on top; place in a Dutch oven (tin plate and all) with lid on; heap live coals of fire on top of lid, and bake until the bacon is done, or to a light crust of brown.

TO BAKE PORK AND BEANS WITHOUT OVEN.

Have a trench 18 inches wide, 18 inches deep, and from 4 to 6 feet long; keep a fire in this for several hours; let fire die down so that there shall be a bed of coals and hot ashes; it is then ready for use. Prepare beans as usual for baking and place in mess kettles; pour in three quarts of hot water; cover with tin plate or mess pan; scrape out the embers until kettle will be near bottom of trench; cover first with ashes, then with coals, and leave undisturbed for six to eight hours. It is a good plan for cooks to soak beans over night and carry them to the next camp. This will permit the furnishing of baked beans at supper while marching.

RICE.

Remember that rice swells very much in boiling, and that a teacupful makes a large dish when cooked. Place in camp kettle, and cover the rice with about two inches of water; boil slowly, or rather simmer, until it is tender, then by gradually slowing the heat let the water evaporate, thus leaving the grains swollen and dry. Rice thus prepared can be used as a vegetable or a pudding by adding salt and pepper in the former and sugar in the latter case.

HOW TO BOIL RICE.

Pick your rice clean and wash it in two cold waters, drawing off the last water just as you are ready to put the rice in the saucepan for boiling. Prepare a saucepan with water sufficient to more than cover the rice by two inches, and in which a little salt has been shaken. The water should be brought to a boil and kept there until it is drained off. When the water is boiling sprinkle in the rice gradually so as not to stop the boiling. Boil for about twenty minutes, keeping the pan covered. Then throw into a colander, covering same; let stand several minutes, this serving a double purpose, allowing rice to drain as well as steam.

Every grain should be found separate and dry.

Remember, boil rapidly from the time you cover the pot until you take it off; this allows each grain to swell to three times its normal size, and the motion prevents the grains from sticking together. Don't stir it, as this will cause it to fall to the bottom and burn.

In order to see if the rice is done, take out one of the grains and crush it between the fingers; if well done it will mash easily and feel perfectly soft.

BAKING-POWDER BISCUITS AND BREAD.

To six quarts of flour add eight tablespoonfuls of baking powder, two spoonfuls salt, and stir thoroughly together; then add about eight tablespoonfuls of clear cold bacon fat; stir again, and add sufficient cold water (never warm water) quickly, and stir to a smooth but not stiff batter. Mix or stir it as little as possible—never knead it—or you will lose the strength (gases) of the powder. Roll or break into equal-sized biscuits; or, best, drop from a large spoon into well-greased pans. Put into a good hot oven, especially hot on top, and bake until done—usually from 15 to 20 minutes, if oven is good.

Never knead the dough, as kneading kills the leavening properties of baking-powder bread. Yeast, or baker's bread, on the other hand, requires much kneading and a good stiff dough. If in a hurry, or inexperienced, biscuits are the most easily made; the great fault in preparing either is not so much inexperience as lack of careful attention to the above details.

BREAD.

In making baking-powder bread observe the same rules as mentioned above; mix into a fairly stiff batter, using a large spoon, not the hands; have your greased pan and hot oven ready; drop or pour the batter into it until about half full, and set into the oven. Get a good even heat below and plenty on top (so as to fill the oven with hot air). When done the loaves will rise to the top of the pan. Bake from 30 to 45 minutes, or until a sliver will pass through the bread and on withdrawal be found dry; if sticky dough adheres to the sliver the bread is not yet done. Regular heat and quick mixing insure most excellent bread in large quantities in an easy way.

FIELD BREAD.

Take five quarts of flour and one and two-thirds tablespoonfuls of yeast powder; mix thoroughly while dry, adding a little salt to suit the taste; then mix in well one tablespoonful of dripping or lard; then add water, and in small quantities at a time, until a biscuit dough is made; knead slightly. Take a Government mess pan and cut off about one inch and a half of the rim, leaving a rough edge. Into this mess pan put dough enough to fill it two-thirds full; cover with another mess pan. A hole should previously have been dug in the ground eighteen or twenty inches in diameter and depth, and a fire burned in it five or six hours. Then take out all the cinders except a bed two or three inches deep; upon this place the mess pans and surround and cover them with hot cinders; over all spread a covering of earth, and leave for five or six hours.

The bread will not burn, as in rising it will not reach the bottom of the upper mess pan. The rough-cut edges of the lower mess pan afford egress to any gases that may be disengaged.

FIELD BREAD, BAKED IN FRYING PAN.

Prepare the dough as above described; grease the frying pan and set it over hot embers until the grease begins to melt; put the dough, rolled to a thickness of half an inch, in the pan and set it on the fire; shake the pan every few moments to prevent the dough from adhering; after the crust has formed on the bottom take the bread out of the pan and set it up on edge, close to the fire, turning it occasionally to insure its being baked through.

PIE CRUST.

To four quarts of flour sift three spoonfuls of baking powder, and a spoonful of salt; add one to two quarts of good bacon fat; cold water enough to make a good stiff dough without kneading. Roll with a bottle to a thin even sheet; line inside of pan—leave sufficient for a covering; cut hole in center of upper crust and bake in hot oven one hour. As a good filling for meat pies, observe the general rules seen in meat stewed, etc., using game and cooked meats if possible.

SUET, OR FIELD PUDDING.

Cut up fine about two quarts of bacon, or salt fat pork, or suet in small disc-shaped pieces. To six quarts of flour add six spoonfuls of baking powder, two quarts of molasses, or one and one-half quarts of sugar, two quarts of currants, raisins, or chopped fruits, one quarter pint of mixed spices. Mix into a good stiff batter with a spoon, and it is ready for the bag and pot. Prepare from a flour bag (inside one) a bag; dip into boiling water and flour well inside, this prevents the pudding from sticking to the bag and absorbing water. Into this bag pour your pudding batter, allowing room for the pudding to swell (be sure of this), and tie up tightly, taking care that no water can get inside of bag. Have boiling two or three boilers of water and drop in your pudding while the water boils; boil two or three hours, according to the size of your pudding.

NOTE.—If the water stops boiling your pudding is spoiled.

To remove the pudding from the bag when done, dip it into a bucket or pan of cold water. It will then slide out easily when the string of the bag is cut. Before putting in the pudding to boil, drop a tin pan or plate into the boiler; this will prevent it from sticking to the bottom of the pot and burning.

PLAIN SAUCE FOR FIELD PUDDING.

To a quart of sugar add a sufficient quantity of hot water and boil, adding a little spice; boil ten minutes, then thicken with flour, stirring continually. Toward the last add a little vinegar until taste is satisfactory. Use more spice or sugar if necessary. Boil until it thickens, and serve separately from pudding. If possible use condensed milk.

STEWED DRIED APPLES.

Pick over the apples carefully; then wash them in cold water and drain. Soak them over night in sufficient cold water to cover them. Put them, with the water in which they have been soaked, into a pot (iron should not be used; an earthenware well-glazed crock or stone jar is preferable); cover closely to simmer until they are tender.

STEWED DRIED PEACHES.

Rules as to cooking, flavoring, etc., for dried apples are applicable to dried peaches.

STEWED DRIED PRUNES.

Pick carefully, wash thoroughly, drain, cover the fruit with cold water and soak thirty minutes.

Proceed then as directed for dried apples. Cook thirty to forty-five minutes only. Longer cooking will break the fruit; this is to be avoided.

They are flavored, served, and can be used as prescribed for dried apples.

CANNED AND DRIED SOUPS.

Many reliable varieties of canned soups are on the market and easily obtainable. The cans contain the directions for preparation.

There are also preparations for dried soups, put up in packages on which are printed directions for preparing.

In preparing articles of the foregoing class the directions, as printed by the manufacturers, should always be followed.

MEAT PIE.
(Sufficient for 22 men.)

16½ pounds meat.	1 pound onions.
5 pounds flour.	2 ounces salt.
1½ pounds suet.	½ ounce pepper.

Make the paste; cut up and stew the onions with jelly from the meat added; cut the meat into dice and place it in a baking dish; add the cooked onions; season with pepper and salt; cover with a light crust, and bake in a quick oven for twenty minutes.

STEW.
(Sufficient for 22 men.)

16½ pounds meat.	1 pound onions.
2 pounds carrots, or other	2 ounces salt,
vegetables.	½ ounce pepper

Cut up the vegetables and onions, which place in the boiler with sufficient water to cover them; add some jelly from the meat; well season with pepper and salt, and stew gently, keeping the lid of the boiler closely shut until the vegetables are tender, then add the meat; let the whole simmer for ten minutes and serve.

SEA PIE.
(Sufficient for 22 men.)

Ingredients the same as for stew, with five pounds of flour and one and one-half pounds of suet or dripping added.

Make the paste; prepare and cook the vegetables and onions as for stew; when the vegetables are tender add the meat; cover the whole over with a light paste, and boil or steam for twenty minutes.

CANNED LIMA BEANS.

Open can one hour before using and empty into bowl. Drain liquor off and cook in boiling water twenty-five minutes. Drain, and add pepper and salt to taste.

CANNED STRING BEANS.

Cook one-half an hour in their own liquor, first cutting in good lengths to look well in dish. When almost done, add salt and pepper. Simmer ten minutes longer and drain off liquor. If can has not enough liquor to cover beans, add water in cooking.

CANNED CORN.

Open can one hour before cooking. Put in kettle and cover with boiling water; let stand ten minutes; drain, and cover corn with hot water, a little salted. Set in vessel of hot water and cook one-half hour. Add pepper and salt, and serve.

CANNED CORN AND TOMATOES, STEWED.

To two cans of tomatoes add one can corn. Stew one-half hour with a little chopped onion; pepper and salt to taste.

SALMON IN CAMP COOKERY.

One pound of salmon, one-pound can of tomatoes; arrange in alternate layers; season with salt, pepper, and two ounces of salt pork cut into dice; add the liquid from both cans and cover the top with powdered hard bread; put a little dripping on top, and bake a light brown.

A CAMP MORSEL.

Take a can of mackerel, salmon, or lobster; chop with raw onion and pickles, and pour vinegar over.

CANNED SALMON, BOILED.

The simplest way of preparing salmon for the table is to open the can, place it in a pan or pot partly full of water, and when quite hot it is ready for the table. No water should be allowed to enter the can as it depreciates the flavor. After the salmon is put on the dish, remove the skin and arrange it as neatly as possible. The liquid in the can should be used for the basis of the sauce with the addition of a little seasoning, and if liked, a little flour for thickening.

CANNED SALMON, DEVILED.

Fry one quarter of an onion until brown; add a gill of water, a teaspoonful each of flour and English mustard, salt and pepper. Simmer and add the liquor from the can of salmon; do not let it burn. Place a pound of salmon (hot) upon a dish, spread the thick sauce over it, and set it in a hot oven a moment to singe the surface.

CANNED SALMON, DANISH MODE.

Peel a dozen medium-sized potatoes; put them in a pan with a little dripping and bake them. When done, arrange a pound of salmon (previously warmed in the tin) in the center of the dish with the potatoes round it; thicken the drippings with a little flour, season it with salt, pepper and a clove of garlic; pour it over the fish and serve.

CANNED CLAM FRITTERS.

1 teacupful flour.	1 teaspoonful baking powder.
½ teaspoonful pepper.	½ teaspoonful salt.

(1 dozen clams chopped; add their liquor.)

Drop from a spoon in hot meat dripping.

CANNED CRAB, DEVILED.

Cut crab meat into small pieces. To six ounces of crab meat mix two ounces of bread crumbs, juice of half a lemon, cayenne pepper and salt. Mix all with milk (condensed), sprinkle fine bread crumbs on top, and color brown in a quick oven.

CANNED LOBSTER, DEVILED.

Prepare the same way as crab, adding a little grated nutmeg to seasoning.

CANNED LOBSTER, STEWED.

Cut the meat up fine and let it boil up once in its own liquor. Add a little pepper and salt, and serve plain or on toast.

CANNED OYSTERS AND MACARONI.

Boil four ounces macaroni in plenty of water, twenty minutes. Cut in pieces one inch long. Put layer of this in bottom of baking dish, a layer of oysters, salt and pepper sprinkled over. Then another layer of macaroni and so on until all is used, having top layer macaroni. Sprinkle grated cheese lightly over top and bake in moderate oven twenty minutes. Serve in same dish.

CANNED OYSTER SAUTÉ.

Drain oysters dry, sprinkle with pepper and roll in flour. Cut one-fourth pound bacon into thin slices, put in frying pan and try out all the fat. Remove bacon and cover bottom of pan with oysters. When brown and crisp on one side, do other side the same. Serve on squares of toast.

TO ROAST (PARCH) COFFEE.

Coffee requires great care and constant attention in roasting—don't leave it to do something else.

Half fill the pan with coffee beans, about fifteen pounds, place it in the oven or on the fire (an even and slow heat is best) and when it gets heated through stir thoroughly from the bottom. Try to stir it so the under berries will come to the top, and vice versa. If fire is quick keep stirring constantly. Use the turnover in stirring, not a spoon. When about half done add half pint of fat or water and stir thoroughly until of a rich brown color, then set off to cool. Some prefer to use the oven and by having heat on top can observe the progress of parching more easily and thoroughly, acting accordingly. Time, about one hour or more to the half-pan full. Great care should be exercised, as good coffee is the backbone of many a meal.

TO MAKE COFFEE.

Into a small coffee boiler, the smallest one, put sufficient cold water for the command, allowing a good quart per man or more; add to it the coffee, ground fine (two quarts ground coffee to fifty men at least), and when the whole boils remove it from the fire, ten minutes before service, to settle.

Another way: First boil the water, then add the coffee: boil ten minutes and remove; boil slowly or it will boil over—a cupful of cold water will prevent it from boiling over when it is boiling too fast, but it must be removed quickly—it will also settle the grounds. Don't ever boil coffee too long as it loses strength, and flavor, and don't be too liberal with the water.

Another way: Allow one heaping tablespoonful of coffee to each pint of water. If five quarts are required put in six or seven quarts of water, thus allowing for evaporation and boiling down. First boil the water, then set the pot near the fire, put in your coffee, let it simmer and boil for thirty minutes on hot ashes and coals, and then set aside close to the fire to keep hot until your meal is ready. A third cup of cold water poured in will clarify it.

TEA.

Scald the pot after each meal. Place the pot close to the fire, but not on it. Allow one heaping teaspoonful of tea for each person. Place it in the pot, and pour in boiling water in sufficient quantity; cover the top securely to retain the heat and aroma, and let it draw for twenty or thirty minutes. It is good either hot or cold.

After tea has been drank at the meal, the old tea leaves may be resteeped, and the tea thus formed can be carried in the canteens. It will be ordinarily better than the water that may be found along the march.

CHAPTER 3

EMBALMED BEEF AND COOKING OVERSEAS: 1898–1912

There had been experiments and trials during the 1890s in an effort to improve the rations, but these had all been based upon war in a climate similar to that in the States. In addition, many of the recommendations had not been made, let alone implemented by 1898 when Congress declared war against Spain. Many of the provisions taken to Cuba would have been very familiar to soldiers of half a century before. The food en route to Cuba was fairly poor, and when the soldiers reached Cuba, transportation issues meant that they did not receive their full rations, added to which the quality of the food was dubious, in particular the beef. In *The Provisioning of the Modern Army in the Field* (1909), the author argued that the failure of the supply departments might be down to the fact that little had been written about subsisting an army since the Civil War, and that the personal experience of officers who had served in small units during the Indian Wars with no experience of large-scale operations, had led to "erroneous notions as to the ease of subsisting armies."

For the Cuba expedition, the meat contract was arranged with meat-packing corporations in Chicago, instead of being procured locally "on the hoof." The "canned roast beef" supplied was most likely the pulp left after the extract had been boiled out of the beef, while much of the "refrigerated beef" shipped to Cuba was so poorly preserved or chemically adulterated that it was dangerous to eat; food poisoning and dysentery caused by the meat resulted in many deaths among American troops weakened in any event by the effects of malaria and yellow fever. During the war 2,500 Americans died of disease—only 345 died as a result of combat. Though the connection was not explicitly made at the time between the meat and the levels of illnesses, a post-war inquiry into the quality of the U.S. Army's food made reference to "embalmed beef," blaming the suppliers for the quality

The 14th Regulars lining up for mess, Palay in the Philippines, 1899. In the foreground a soldier grinds coffee while in the background the men line up for their meal. (US Quartermaster Corps, NARA)

of the meat. One army medical officer described the refrigerated beef: "[M]uch of the beef I examined arriving on the transports from the United States ... [was] apparently preserved by injected chemicals to aid deficient refrigeration," the medical officer wrote. "It looked well, but had an odor similar to that of a dead human body after being injected with formaldehyde, and it tasted when first cooked like decomposed boric acid ..." It was suggested that the canned meat was the residue from other processes. These claims were supported by other officers, including Theodore Roosevelt (who had ordered an entire batch of the rancid beef be thrown overboard on the voyage to Cuba). In return the packers claimed that illnesses were due to the way the meat had been handled in the field kitchens. While the inquiry noted that these products were bought by the public and used by the Navy without issue, and drew attention to deficiencies in the transport, the newspapers seized on the subject, and the "embalmed-beef scandal" contributed to the resignation of the Secretary of War.

The rations enjoyed by American troops during the Philippine Insurrection seem to have been of better quality than in Cuba, while foraging there helped soldiers broaden their diet, though some soldiers reported ill effects from local produce. In 1900, American troops were deployed from the Philippines, and later from the States, to join the China Relief Expedition. In the report on the expedition, General Chaffee noted that: "Capt. Frank DeW. Ramsey, Ninth Infantry, chief commissary and quartermaster with the troops, has quite successfully managed the timely arrival of supplies. At no time have the troops seriously suffered for food. We have not, of course, been able to issue in full the vegetable component of the ration."

The Spanish-American War made clear that the War Department needed reform, as did its constituent departments, and major reorganization followed, including the establishment of the General Staff and War College. Reforms were clearly required in the Subsistence and Quartermaster departments, especially to take into account the varying climates in which the U.S. Army was now operating. The end result of the reforms following the war resulted in the consolidation of the Subsistence, Pay, and Quartermaster's departments into the Quartermaster Corps in 1912.

The 1910 *Manual for the Subsistence Department* was intended for distribution to officers of the department. This section on rations demonstrates the progress made on providing appropriate rations to troops in a wide variety of environments and situations. The level of detail on beef has increased considerably since the 1902 edition!

Overleaf: US Army cooks, 1909.

Manual for the Subsistence Department, United States Army (1910)

Article V. RATIONS.

145. The garrison ration is for troops in garrison, on the march, and in camp; the field ration is for troops in the field in active campaign, with sufficient transportation; the haversack ration for troops in the field in active campaign, when transportation is limited; the travel ration for troops traveling otherwise than by marching, and separated from cooking facilities; the emergency ration for troops in time of war in active campaign for use on occasions of emergency, and the Filipino ration is prescribed for Philippine Scouts, whether in garrison, in the field, or traveling. When impracticable for Philippine Scouts to use the Filipino ration while traveling other than by marching, on account of the lack of cooking facilities or for other reasons, the regular travel ration may be prescribed. Ordinarily it is not intended that the field or haversack ration will be used, except in time of war beyond the advance supply depots where accountability ceases. If at any time use is made of the haversack or other form of ration on which no savings are allowed, the articles forming such ration will be dropped on special abstracts approved by the commanding officer.

FRESH BREAD.

146. Fresh bread is supplied to troops in garrison from post bakeries operated in accordance with Army Regulations. In the field, if the garrison ration is furnished as authorized in permanent camps, bakeries will be established whenever practicable and operated in like manner as bakeries at posts.

147. When the field or haversack ration is furnished, and troops are in active campaign, bakeries will be established when practicable. The commissary will furnish the flour and yeast rations due troops direct to the field bakeries, any amounts in excess of those required to furnish full allowance of bread to troops being retained by the commissary. If other stores are needed in baking bread, they will be furnished by the commissary to the bakery upon properly approved requisitions.

FRESH BEEF.

148. As usually furnished in the United States, hind quarters include one rib. When so cut, and trimmed according to specifications, the difference in weight between fore and hind quarters will not exceed 25 pounds per carcass. To comply with specifications, the proportion of fore and hind quarter meat to be delivered should be about as 13 to 12 for average size steers.

149. "Kidney fat" includes all the fat pertaining to and immediately surrounding the kidneys, and does not include other suet in the hind quarters.

150. A study of the following rules will enable a commissary or inspector to see that the meat delivered is according to specifications as to quality, condition, and sex:

Both dark-red lean meat and yellow fat generally indicate age, though some young animals have a decidedly yellow fat due to peculiarities of breed, character of feed, etc. Light-red lean meat and white fat indicate youth. The marrow in the bones of a young animal is soft and red, and that in an old animal is hard and light in color. Soft, white, and wide cartilage indicates a young animal, while hard, dark, and thin cartilage indicates an old animal. Looking along the backbone the character of the cartilage between the vertebrae can be determined. This cartilage generally becomes hard at the age of 6 or 7 years. The cartilage of the breastbone becomes hard in an old animal.

In the female the size and condition of the udder show the relative age. The udder of the heifer shows a clean cut and a firm, uniform mass in either flank, while that of the cow presents a more or less flabby appearance. Sometimes the udder of an old cow is removed, some fat taken from a steer substituted therefor, and the flank is skewered over in such a way as to resemble the udder of a heifer. The presence of skewers in the udder should arouse suspicion, and the appearance of the rest of the carcass should give conclusive proof of this deception.

The carcass of a bull shows massive shoulders, thick bulging neck, and broad breast. It shows a more rounded rump and has darker and coarser meat than a steer, cow, or heifer. In the case of the bull there is an absence of scrotal fat. The fore quarters of a bull are relatively larger than his hind quarters.

The carcass of a steer should show youth. Its flesh should be florid in color and firm and elastic to the touch and lighter in color than that of a cow. Its most distinctive feature is a bunch of fat known as the "cod," which is enveloped in the scrotum.

In all male carcasses the section of the pelvic or "rump" bone shown in the hind quarter is more or less curved. At the outer end of this section is a crescent-shaped piece of lean meat sometimes separated from the end of the bone by a little fat. In the fore quarter of a steer in good condition the surface of the cut separating the fore from the hind quarter should show the lean meat well mottled with fat; while that of a cow shows little, if any, mottling. Each rib of a steer, as shown in the fore quarter, generally presents a well-rounded appearance, while in the fore quarter of a cow each rib presents a surface more or less flattened.

In female carcasses the section of the pelvic or "rump" bone, as shown in the hind quarter, is nearly straight, the decrease in curvature depending on the number of calves born to the female. At the outer end of this section no lean meat is visible. A spayed heifer's carcass generally shows the scar in the flank.

Excessive moisture, which is mostly observed in flanks, abdomen, under the shoulder blade, and at the brisket, in the order named, is particularly noticeable in the carcasses of old cows or any animal that is ill-conditioned.

151. At each post at which a veterinarian is stationed and which is supplied with fresh beef by local dealers from cattle slaughtered in the vicinity, the commanding officer, whenever it is possible to do so, will cause the veterinarian to inspect the cattle before they are slaughtered and at the time of slaughtering, and also the beef when delivered at the post, with a view of determining whether the contract requirements have been met, and to report in writing to the commanding officer the result of such inspection.

BEEF CATTLE.

152. Before accepting beef cattle a commissary, or board of officers if convened for the purpose, should be satisfied as to their age, sex, quality, and health. A veterinarian will assist in the inspection whenever practicable.

153. *Age.*—The age of cattle is estimated by the teeth. The adult animal has 8 incisor teeth in the front of the lower jaw, but none in the upper jaw, which is callous. At 2 years of age the middle 2 permanent incisors are generally well up, having replaced the "milk teeth" present at birth. The remaining permanent incisors appear in pairs at irregular intervals, the complete set generally being fully developed at 4 years of age. After that, age can only be estimated by the wear of the teeth and the general appearance of the jaw. As age advances the teeth become more and more worn and yellowish, are not so crowded in the jaw, and lose their chisel shape, the gums at the same time receding.

The age of cattle may also be roughly guessed at by the horns. When 3 years old they are smooth and handsome. At 5 a ring generally appears on the horns of steers at their roots, and a new ring appears each succeeding year. These rings are, however, not well defined and are liable to be tampered with, as they can be filed off, and are therefore not a reliable guide.

Cattle for army use should be between 2 and 6 years of age.

154. *Sex.*—A bull is an uncastrated male.

A bullock is a young bull.

A steer is a male not full grown and castrated when young.

An ox is a full-grown male castrated when young.

A stag is a male castrated late in life.

A heifer is a young female.

A maiden heifer is an adult female which has not been allowed to breed.

A spayed heifer is a female, with ovaries removed.

A cow is a female that has had a calf.

155. *Quality.*—The most suitable steers are those which are moderately fat. Very fat animals, whose flesh wastes much in cooking, are as much to be avoided as those which are thin and underfed.

A good steer should have a level, straight back, and its bones should be well covered with flesh.

A fine, soft, mellow, elastic, and movable skin is a point of excellence.

156. *Condition.*—In examining a herd of cattle, the following points may be taken as indicative of good health:

Movements brisk, eyes bright and full, muzzle cool and moist; dung normal, neither watery, hard, nor blood-stained; coat glossy.

The animals should, when quiet, be constantly chewing the cud; if lying down, should, when quietly raised, stretch themselves.

The following points indicate ill health:

Movements dull and sluggish, eyes dull and hollow, muzzle hot and dry, heat at base of horns, dull coat, tight skin.

Should an animal not stretch himself on being quietly raised, or not chew the cud for any length of time, or stand apart from his fellows, or cower behind a bush or wall, he must be looked upon with suspicion and should be rejected.

157. *Purchase.*—Beef cattle will be purchased only when necessary for supplying beef to troops in campaign or on the march.

The local resources of invaded territory in the way of fresh meat should always be utilized. The animals brought in by foraging parties will be assembled in corrals established on the line of communications, and the slaughtering (under the observation of veterinarians) and issuing will generally be conducted by commissary officers.

In regions distant from railroad or water communication and deficient in local supplies, it may be necessary to purchase herds of cattle in advance of a movement, driving them with the command and slaughtering them as needed. Such purchases will be made by contract when practicable. If time or circumstances render open-market purchases necessary, and do not permit, of reducing to writing the terms of purchase agreed upon, the method to be used in determining the net weight will be stated to, and accepted by, the parties supplying the cattle.

158. *Contracts.*—Contracts for beef cattle are made on the form furnished by the Subsistence Department for the purpose. This form provides for the purchase of steers only, excluding those that are wild, lame, or diseased. It specifies the maximum and minimum limits of age and weight, generally 6 and 2 years, and 1,400 and 1,000 pounds, respectively, and prescribes the method of determining the weight and of making deliveries as follows:

If practicable, the cattle shall be weighed; in which case they shall be kept twelve hours, immediately before weighing, without food or water. Their net weight shall be considered as 55 per cent of the gross weight when the animal weighs 1,300 pounds or more; 50 per cent when weighing between 1,300 and 800 pounds; and 40 per cent when weighing 800 pounds or less.

If impracticable to weigh the cattle, the herd will be separated into three lots, according to apparent weight—heavy, medium, light—or into a greater number of lots, if the herd is large and the cattle of great diversity in weight. From each lot an animal will be selected as of the average weight and condition thereof, killed and dressed and trimmed as follows: Necks cut off perpendicularly to the line of the vertebrae, leaving but three cervical vertebrae on the carcass, shanks of fore quarters cut off 4 inches above the point where the long bone (radius) makes a joint with the knee, shanks of hind quarters cut off 8 inches above the point where the long bone (tibia) makes a joint with the uppermost bone of the hock. The actual scale weight of the carcass of each animal thus dressed and trimmed (excluding necks, shanks, and kidney fat) shall be considered as the average net weight of the cattle of the lot from which the animal was taken.

The delivery of the beef cattle shall be accomplished in the following manner:

When the contractor is ready to deliver the cattle he should so notify the commissary. If there be a commanding officer the commissary shall at once report such notification to him. Thereupon the commanding officer shall immediately convene a board of officers, to consist of as many members, not exceeding three, as can be assembled, one of whom shall be the commissary, and the others preferably company commanders. Whenever practicable, the board will be assisted by a veterinarian. The commissary and the commanding officer shall comprise the board if no other officers are available. As soon as practicable, the board shall personally inspect the cattle, select such as conform to the requirements of the contract, and determine their net weight in the manner prescribed in the preceding paragraphs. Upon the determination of. such net weight the commissary shall receive the cattle so selected and plainly brand them on the left hind quarter with the letters "U. S." If the commissary be the only officer available, he shall at once pursue the course prescribed in this paragraph for a board of officers. The board shall furnish a report (or the commissary shall furnish a certificate, as the case may be) setting forth fully the method pursued in determining the net weight of the selected cattle, the several steps taken by them or him in the performance of their or his whole duty relating to the contract, and the number of head and aggregate net weight of the selected cattle.

159. *Care.*—In driving cattle they should be started on the road at daybreak, and after one hour they should be stopped to rest and ruminate when they will be found to drive with more ease to themselves than if the stoppage had not been made. At meridian, if opportunity offers, the herd should be halted from one to two hours, allowing them to feed and water. Cattle should never be driven, but permitted to assume their own gait, except the lively fast-traveling ones, which should be held in check to give those in rear an opportunity to close up and prevent separation. A herd should never be separated in sections, especially in proceeding through a wooded country. The number of men required in the field is about 3 to the 100 head. They should be placed at equal distances on the sides, with a strong force of herders in the rear to guard against straggling, for there will be in all large herds some that are lame or too heavy to travel well.

In herding cattle where there are no fences for corrals the cattle should be allowed a free range of country, with mounted herders at equal intervals and within sight of each other on the outer circle.

In pasturing cattle water should be of convenient access from the feeding grounds, and cattle should not be kept on the pasture more than eight hours in twenty-four, commencing at daylight in the morning, removed at the expiration of four hours, and replaced, say, at 2 o'clock p.m., and removed at

6 o'clock p.m. This method gives them an opportunity to chew the cud, and prevents unnecessary trampling of the grass.

When sufficient pasturage can not be secured for beeves, hay, corn, and other articles of forage will be purchased and fed to them in such quantities as may be necessary. Hay and corn are the best forage, and if fed in proportions of about 12 pounds of each will ordinarily keep cattle in good condition—to be fed half each in the morning and half in the evening.

Cattle should be allowed to drink whenever they desire, but when this is not possible, they should be driven to water after the morning and evening feed.

Cattle should be salted twice a week with about 4 ounces per head at each issue.

160. *Slaughtering.*—Roughly, one butcher is required for every thousand troops, A veterinarian should be present, whenever practicable, when the animals are killed and dressed. The animal heat leaves the beef in about twenty-four hours after being killed, and if an animal is killed, dressed, and immediately thereafter issued to troops it is very liable to cause diarrhea and is otherwise prejudicial to health. For this reason beef cattle should be slaughtered late in the day, if practicable, to allow the animal heat to escape over night. In temperate climates cattle should, when practicable, be killed twenty-four hours before issue; in hot climates at least ten hours. Cattle should be deprived of food for twelve hours before slaughter.

In taking off hides care should be observed not to cut them, as every knife cut reduces the value of a hide. Hides will be preserved by drying or salting, and sold as soon as practicable.

Whenever time and convenience will permit, the tallow will be rendered, placed in suitable receptacles, and sold as soon as practicable.

161. *Accounting.*—Beeves will be accounted for by number and net weight on the return of subsistence stores, hides by number, and tallow by pounds.

CHAPTER 4

COOKING IN A GLOBAL WAR:
WORLD WAR I

I n 1905, the first school for military bakers and cooks was opened at Fort Riley. This was the fulfilment of one of the recommendations of the 1875 *Report on the Hygiene of the United States Army,* which had been repeated at regular intervals by Commissaries-General ever since. Lucius Holbrook commanded the school until 1911, and during his time there he wrote several manuals for army bakers and mess officers. He invented the first army field oven, which he was able to test when he was commander of the bakeries with Pershing's Mexican Expeditionary Force in 1916. That year the War Department issued the *Manual for Army Cooks* (a revision of the 1910 manual) and a *Manual for Army Bakers* in 1916.

In 1907 the development work done on rations after the Spanish-American War led to the creation of Emergency Rations—intended to be carried in a soldier's pocket in the field, and used only when field rations were unavailable. These emergency rations comprised three slabs of parched wheat and meat powder, three of sweetened chocolate, and packages of salt and pepper. Both the meat and sweet cakes could be eaten out of the can, plus the chocolate could be made into a drink, and the meat cake could be cooked in several ways. These emergency rations would accompany the American Expeditionary Force to the Western Front in 1917. Two other new types of ration were introduced to the AEF in France; the Trench Ration and the Reserve Ration. The Trench Ration, which could feed twenty-five men for a day, was designed in response to the use of gas on the front lines, which could contaminate food prepared in field kitchens. It comprised mainly canned foods, sealed in a large, galvanized can as protection against gas. Introduced slightly later, the Reserve (or "Iron") Ration was designed for an individual soldier who was away from a garrison or field kitchen. Its contents would have been familiar to soldiers of an older generation: bacon or canned meat, usually corned beef, hard bread or hardtack, coffee, sugar, and salt. The can was cylindrical and weighed one pound, which did not prove practical. Although the American Garrison Ration, as detailed in the manual below, was probably the best (and definitely the most calorific) enjoyed by any soldier during the war, complaints about food, particularly about the canned meat, were common throughout the war.

Opposite: Baking bread for Pershing's army near Namiquipa, Mexico in 1916. The first use of new field kitchens. (Library of Congress)

Manual for Army Cooks (1916)

Chapter II

The Garrison Ration

COMPONENTS OF THE RATION.

199. **Beef.**—It is the most important as well as the most expensive article of the ration, its value being about equal to all the other components combined. It is the foundation of the ration and careless handling will soon put an organization in debt, while if it is handled carefully substantial savings may be made with which to purchase pork, chicken, and other meats not included in the ration. The organization commander should pay particular attention to the beef and flour components, which taken together amount to more than one-half the value of the ration.

200. **Soup.**— A good stock soup should be prepared daily for dinner and served in a course by itself, before the more substantial portion of the meal. Serve plenty of croutons or crackers with it, seeing that it is hot when served and that the grease is skimmed off. Soup stock should be made fresh every day or two. Cut the fresh meat into small pieces, break or saw the bones and place them together in cold water for several hours, then put on range and allow to simmer for about six hours. After about two hours of simmering the juices will be extracted from the meat. The meat should then be removed from the boiler before the fibers have become hard and indigestible, and placed in a cool place for use in hash, meat balls, etc. The grease rises to the top and forms a crust which may easily be removed and placed in the drip pan. The stock when prepared should be poured into another receptacle and cooled. The stock boiler should then be cleaned out and a new start made. Beef stock is not only used in making soup, but in hash, stews, gravies, pot pies, etc.

The average cook does not seem to realize that he has more opportunity to show his skill in preparing a good appetizing soup than in most other dishes. Seasoning such as can be obtained from a judicious use of different kinds of pepper, celery, bacon, or parsley and a substantial filling of different vegetables will produce a dish which the men will enjoy as much as any part of the meal.

201. **Bread and flour**.—This is the cheapest component of the ration, considering the nutritive value, and consequently the greater the quantity used, the less expensive will be the mess. At least 10 per cent should be saved on this component after buying the flour and bread used in the kitchen. This saving should be used for the purchase of breakfast foods for which no allowance is given. Bread should not be cut until just before it is to be used and then in thin slices, which should be piled close together in order to prevent it from drying out. It should be purchased in small quantities as required from day to day. Bread left over should be piled in the form of the loaf before it was cut, covered with a cloth, put in the bread box and served first at the next meal. All crumbs and pieces of dried bread not desirable for the table should be saved and placed in a flour sack and allowed to dry out. It may then be toasted and ground for use in place of cracker crumbs or in preparing croquettes, meat balls, etc. Milk toast and bread puddings should be served often enough to use up the remainder of the dried bread.

The flour should be used in the preparation of biscuits, pancakes, hot rolls, and desserts. Bread and rolls that have dried out may be greatly freshened by moistening and placing in a slow oven for half an hour. Place a moistened flour sack or dish towel in the bottom of a bake pan so that the ends may be folded over the bread or rolls, or place a pan of boiling water in the bottom of the oven and the pan of bread or rolls on the top shelf without a cloth, leaving the oven door on the second notch. The bread should be allowed to remain in a 20-count oven for about 20 minutes.

Hard bread which is ordered sold to the troops to prevent its accumulating may be toasted and used in soups, chowder, bread puddings, etc.

Corn meal should be served occasionally as a mush, fried or in corn bread.

202. **Baking powder**.—The allowance is sufficient for one mess of pancakes, biscuits, etc, each day. Usually about one-half as much of a more expensive baking powder is required. In using baking powder remember that it, with the other ingredients, should be mixed with cold water or milk and used at once. This is because the action of water on the ingredients in the powder causes the carbonic gas, which makes the dough light and spongy, to form and escape. If the mixture is not used at once it should be kept cool, otherwise this gas will escape and the results will be unsatisfactory. The best rule is to use at once after mixing.

Recipe for baking powder.—A very good baking powder can be made as follows: Take 16 ounces of cream of tartar, 8 ounces baking soda and 4 ounces of corn starch and mix thoroughly by putting through a sieve at least nine times.

203. **The bean** component is one of the most important. Beans and peas contain much muscle-building material and with the right proportion of fat added in the form of bacon (about 20 per cent), are equal to meat in food value, and are a suitable substitute for fresh beef. The variety of beans served should be as great as possible. The best results are obtained by soaking the beans three hours, pouring off the water, scalding them in a second water which is poured off, boiling them an hour in a third water, then allowing them to simmer until done. This gives the beans a more agreeable flavor than if the water is not changed.

For an organization of 100 men the maximum amount of dried vegetables to be used in a 30-day period even during the season when fresh vegetables are not plentiful is as follows:

Issue beans, 200 pounds. This is sufficient for five messes of baked beans, three messes of stewed beans, and three soups.

Dried peas, 60 pounds. This will make three messes of stewed peas.

Lima beans, 60 pounds. This is sufficient for three messes of stewed beans.

Kidney beans, 45 pounds. This is sufficient for three messes of stewed beans.

Chili beans, 50 pounds. This will furnish sufficient beans for two meals of chili con carne and two of stewed beans. When served as a vegetable, add five pounds of bacon.

Rice, about 70 pounds. This should supply three meals of boiled rice, three of curry and rice, and about two puddings and leave sufficient for soups.

Dried sweet corn, 40 pounds. This is sufficient for three messes of stewed corn and three of soup. It takes up very readily about twice its weight of water and can be prepared in about 50 minutes.

Hominy, 30 pounds. This is sufficient for three messes. Should be served as a vegetable, boiled, with diced bacon added. It may be boiled and, when cold, sliced, fried, and served with sirup. The canned lye hominy is much enjoyed by the men when fried brown in ham or bacon fat and served at breakfast.

204. **Vegetables** consist of potatoes, onions, and canned tomatoes. The allowance of vegetables is ample during the winter months, while during the season of fresh vegetables a considerable saving should be made. This saving may be used for the purchase of fresh garden truck, or when a company garden is provided should be added to the general mess fund. During the winter and early spring the mess will derive great benefit from the dried vegetables mentioned in the preceding paragraph.

Onions and tomatoes are most valuable as seasoning components. They may be served as a vegetable about once in five days. Tomatoes are chiefly used in soups and stews and onions in Hamburg steaks, salads, etc.

Potatoes should be stored in a cool dry place. Warmth and moisture hasten decay and promote the growth of sprouts. Sprouts should be removed as soon as they appear, as this growth exhausts the nutritive value of the potato. After peeling and until used, the potato should be kept covered with cold water, exposure to the air causing them to become dark and tough. Fermentation is likely to start if the potatoes are left in warm water. Keep them cool.

All potatoes left over should be used up in the form of fried potatoes, in meat balls, hash, soups, and salads.

All left-over vegetables should be cooled and placed in the ice box in warm weather. This applied to potatoes, beans, and salads in particular. Ferments thrive in temperatures above 70° F. The careless cook, may, through neglect, cause stomach trouble in warm weather.

Cabbage is invaluable in the season when fresh vegetables can not be procured. It contains a certain per cent of sulphur and while cooking it should be submerged in water, which absorbs the sulphur.

Parsnips, turnips, beets, and *carrots* are all valuable for a change during the winter months. If purchasing with the intention of storing for winter use they should be well matured; otherwise they will not keep.

205. **Dried fruits**.—Excellent recipes are given in this manual for handling dried fruits, and the entire allowance should be consumed in the mess unless fresh fruit is abundant and cheap enough to be purchased from the savings. The acids in fruit are desirable in a well regulated diet. The quantity of fruit allowed is based upon ordinary requirements.

The dried fruits issued are easily prepared for the table. The men tire of them when they are prepared as stews too often. They should be prepared as butter and used as fillings for pies, rolls, cobblers, plum duffs, etc.

The following recipe, by Lieut. Col. Wilkins, Quartermaster Corps, has furnished excellent results:

1. Thoroughly wash the evaporated fruit in about three waters.

2. Cover with plenty of water and soak over night.

3. Stew slowly until tender.

4. Rub through a colander and add to each pound of dried fruit used three-fourths of a pound of sugar, one teaspoonful of cloves, two teaspoonsful of cinnamon, and a little vinegar.

206. **Coffee**.—The use of tea and coffee to the exclusion of water is a great mistake. The quantity of the coffee component consumed will be greatly reduced if plenty of cold water is placed on the table where the men can help themselves. If good coffee is made the allowance is hardly sufficient. The use of tea, however, decreases the consumption.

Allow coffee to boil not over five minutes, then reduce to a simmering temperature. Do not allow it to boil violently enough to permit the air to carry off the aroma which gives the coffee its agreeable flavor. If boiled for more than five minutes the tannic acid is extracted and forms injurious compounds which irritate the membranes of the stomach. The grounds should not be allowed to accumulate for more than three meals—better two—before the pot is scoured and cleaned.

Tea is a very good substitute for coffee and should be used for dinner and supper, iced in summer. It has about the same physical effect as coffee, but is lighter and less bulky.

In preparing tea it is well to clean it by pouring over it boiling water, then put the leaves in boiling water and allow to draw for about five minutes just before serving. Do not allow to stand longer in the hot water. About three-fourths of an ounce per gallon of water is sufficient for strong tea, one-half ounce for medium strong. Tea should not be allowed to stand in tin vessels, even for a short time, on account of the action of tannic acid on the metal.

207. **Sugar** is a cheap article of diet, considering its high nutritive value. Next to fat and oil it furnishes the most complete food for heat and energy. It is a quick-acting food and relieves exhaustion very rapidly. It should be placed on the table and the men should be allowed to help themselves. When this method is used the consumption will increase for a short time, but soon adjusts itself when properly supervised. The mess sergeant should take care to see that none is left in the bottom of the cups after the coffee is drunk.

Granulated sugar makes an excellent sirup for table use; it is cheaper than other sirup and the men prefer it to cheap grades.

208. **Milk**.—The allowance is based upon the requirements for coffee only. If used directly in the coffee there is sufficient for use twice daily.

209. **Seasonings**.—*Flavoring extracts.*—The allowance is about sufficient, any excess used or savings made will affect the cash credit very little. Sugar, salt, bacon, ham, onions, parsnips, carrots, pepper, garlic, mustard, herbs, spices, lemons, and many other articles are used for flavoring food.

210. **Butter and oleomargarine.**— The allowance, one-half ounce per man per day, is sufficient for hot cakes, rolls, or biscuits. It should be served individually.

211. **Lard and lard substitute.**—The cash credit of this component is sufficient. The suet from beef and all surplus fat received should be carefully rendered. This with the grease skimmed from stock, soups, and gravies will furnish most of the shortening, drippings, etc., required in the kitchen. A pan or kettle in which the suet is rendered should be kept on the stove and all fat should be placed in it. The grease which gathers on the stock or on gravies, etc., should be skimmed off and placed in this pan. Each evening the grease which has accumulated in the suet pan is strained off into a jar or other receptacle and placed in a cool place. This accumulation which is called drippings can be used for frying, either deep or shallow, and can be used in rolls or pastry when carefully strained. Lard, however, is better for the latter.

212. **Desserts.**—The ration contains all the material necessary for supplying a dessert each day. The recipes given herein provide a sufficient variety. The dessert is usually one of the cheapest components of the meal and should be given at dinner and frequently at supper. The men enjoy it, especially on bean day, when a good plum duff is much relished by those who do not care for beans.

A good sauce should be provided for puddings. It costs little and is well liked. One gallon is sufficient for about 25 men.

☙

Overleaf: World War I recruiting poster for army bakers and cooks. (Library of Congress)

Chapter IV

The Elementary Principles of Cooking and the Elements of Nutrition

249. **Preparation of food**, or proper cooking, has much to do with the nutritive value. Cooking changes food into more soluble forms and renders it more nutritious and appetizing. The application of the heat necessary for cooking destroys any disease germs, parasites, and dangerous organisms that the food may contain. This applies to both animal and vegetable food. The cooking of meat brings out the flavor and odor of the extractives and softens the gelatinoids of the connective tissues, making the meat more tender. Extreme heat, however, has a tendency to harden the lean portions (albuminoids) and decrease the flavor.

Meats lose weight in cooking, mainly through the loss of water. The nutritive value of beef soup depends upon the substances dissolved by the water out of the meat, bones, and gristle.

In many vegetables the valuable portions (carbohydrates) are contained in tiny cells with thick walls on which the digestive juices have little effect. The heat of cooking ruptures these walls and makes the starch more soluble. The heat tends also to produce agreeable flavors by changing the starch into sugar.

Flour is made more palatable in the form of bread, cake, and pastry through the use of compressed air, yeast, or baking powder.

Scrupulous cleanliness should always be observed in handling, keeping, and serving the food. This is most important for the sake of health. Cleanliness in handling food not only consists in personal cleanliness, the cleanliness of utensils, kitchen equipment, etc., but also freedom from undesirable bacteria, other minute organisms, worms, and parasites. *Food, raw or cooked, should be kept scrupulously clean*, whether in the market, the cart, or the storeroom; otherwise it is likely to be contaminated. *Infected water, milk, oysters, and certain vegetables* have been known to spread typhoid, cholera, scarlet fever, and diphtheria, thus bringing sickness and death to large numbers of people.

Meats may also contain parasites such as tapeworms in beef, pork, and mutton, also trichinae in pork, which are always injurious to the health.

Vegetables, too, have been known to become contaminated with the eggs of parasites, due to certain garden fertilizers.

Raw fruits and vegetables should always be thoroughly cleaned before eating. The heat of cooking is usually sufficient to destroy all dangerous organisms.

250. **Methods of cooking**.—The object to be attained will often decide the manner of cooking. For example, in roasting meat we desire to retain the juices within. Hence the meat is placed in a very hot oven to seal the pores and prevent the escape of the juices, the oven being reduced to a lower temperature when the meat has been thoroughly browned.

To make beef stock, first place the bones and fresh meat in cold water for some time, as the juices of the bones and meat are readily extracted in this manner. The process is hastened by the addition of a little salt.

To make a stew or potpie, a part of the meat juices should be retained in the meat and a part in the surrounding liquid; hence we place the meat in cold water and bring it to a boil as soon as possible in order to seal the pores after a certain amount of the juice has been extracted.

To get the best results in boiling beef, it is necessary to retain the juices within the meat. For this reason the water is made to boil briskly before the meat is introduced. Upon contact with the hot water the pores are sealed. The temperature is then lowered and the cooking continued at a simmering point.

Size of articles.—The time required for cooking any article depends upon its size; consequently, when several pieces of meat are roasted in the same pan, or when potatoes are baked together in the same oven, an effort should be made to have them about the same size.

Reason for uniform texture.—It is owing to the maintenance of an even temperature in the presence of moisture that it is possible to make bread, cakes, meat balls, fritters, etc., of the same texture throughout, while a thin brown crust is formed on the surface. It has been shown by the use of a maximum thermometer that while the temperature of a baking oven is about 450° F., the temperature within a loaf of bread while baking never rises appreciably above 212° F., the highest temperature of free steam.

251. **Temperature of baking, etc**.—Frequently too little attention is paid to the proper temperature of the oven and to the general character of the meat or other articles to be cooked. For example, a temperature that is exactly right for browning a roast will ruin a fruit cake in a few minutes. To roast properly a tough piece of meat requires a "slow" oven and much time in order to permit the heat to penetrate to the center, thoroughly dissolving and breaking down the tissues, thus making it tender, while a small piece of meat can be roasted in a "quick oven." It is this principle of slow cooking in a moderately low

temperature for a long period that renders the fireless cooker so much superior to anything else for certain kinds of work, especially that of cooking tough meat until it is tender.

To determine the temperature of an oven.—A good practical method of determining the temperature of an oven is to insert the hand well into it and count the number of seconds that you are able to keep it there. In counting, repeat moderately slowly 0–1000, 1–1000, 2–1000, and the small numbers indicated will correspond very closely to the number of seconds. The burning sensation experienced about the roots of the nails is sufficiently uniform to the experienced cook to render this a reliable method. It is followed by the experienced chef and should be by the student cook. If the temperature of the oven is somewhat greater than anticipated, food will often have the appearance of being well done, when, as a matter of fact, the cooking has barely begun. For this reason a cook should have some idea as to the "times" of cooking, as well as to oven temperatures.

252. **Table of oven temperatures** as determined by the hand-second counts:

	First counts	Count after browning	Time
Meats:			
Beef roast, 5-pound pieces	10	18	1½ to 2½ hours.
Mutton roast, 5-pound pieces	12	20	2 to 2½ hours.
Pork roast, 5-pound pieces	15	20	2 to 3½ hours.
Veal roast, 5-pound pieces	12	18	2½ to 3 hours.
Venison roast, 5-pound pieces	12	18	2½ to 3 hours.
Turkey roast, 12 pounds each	12	18	2 to 3½ hours.
Chicken roast, 3 pounds each	12	18	1½ hours.
Duck roast, 3 pounds each	12	18	1½ hours.
Salmon hash	12	16	1 to 1½ hours.

Vegetables:

Beans	15	30	12 hours.
Carrots	15	17	1 hour.
Parsnips	15	17	40 to 60 minutes.
Potatoes, baked	12	15	30 to 40 minutes.
Potatoes, browned	10	15	20 to 30 minutes.
Potatoes, cheesed	15	18	40 minutes.
Potatoes, hashed	12	15	30 minutes.
Potatoes, Lyonnaise	12	15	30 minutes.
Potatoes, sweet	15	17	30 to 60 minutes.
Squash	15	17	30 to 40 minutes.

Breads:

Braided bread, 2-ounce	12	14	20 to 25 minutes.
Cinnamon rolls, 2-ounce	10	12	10 to 15 minutes.
Jenny Linds, 16-ounce	18	20	30 to 40 minutes.
Muffins, 2-ounce	15	15	20 to 30 minutes.
Parkerhouse rolls, 2-ounce	10	12	10 to 15 minutes.
Raisin buns, 2-ounce	15	18	35 to 40 minutes.
Sandwich buns, 2-ounce	10	12	10 to 15 minutes.
Tea buns, 2-ounce	15	18	35 to 40 minutes.
French bread, 18-ounce	14	30	40 minutes.

Cakes:

Apple, 16-ounce (6 by 10 inches)	15	15	20 to 30 minutes.
Coffee, 16-ounce (6 by 10 inches)	15	15	15 to 20 minutes.
Apple kutchen, 16-ounce	15	18	25 to 30 minutes.

253. **Cold is used in preventing fermentation**, hence is a preservative of food. We constantly make use of this fact by placing butter, milk, meats, etc., in the ice box; by storing certain vegetables and fruits in root cellars and pits in the ground; by preserving yeast in a cool place; and by stopping the further proving (rising) of dough, so that it shall not be ready to bake before the oven is ready to receive it. Fresh meat will keep better in a moderately cool, dry place than in a damp ice box at a much lower temperature. Should hot weather require the use of the ice box, the meat should not come in contact with the walls or with the ice.

Cold water keeps fresh vegetables from wilting. It quickly restores such garden truck as radishes, lettuce, onions, etc., that have been exposed to the sun after gathering or have been left in a warm temperature for a time, rendering them fresh, crisp, and wholesome. Potatoes and turnips that have been peeled must be placed in cold water to keep them crisp and to prevent them from becoming discolored and tough. If cooked while wilted and discolored they retain their discoloration and toughness to a considerable extent.

Cold water draws out certain undesirable flavors when vegetables and certain canned, barreled, or dried fish and meats are submerged in it. It also extracts the juices from meats and bones. This process is hastened by the addition of a small quantity of salt.

254. **Flavors.**—Food should possess decided flavors without being too highly seasoned. It should be served hot or cold as intended. Generally we like our tea, coffee, cooked vegetables, and meats served hot, while we prefer our drinking water, butter, salads, fresh fruits, such garden truck as lettuce, radishes, and onions, and many of our desserts served cold. Many components of a meal that are lukewarm instead of decidedly hot or cold are most unappetizing.

255. **Seasoning.**—Cooks must not be satisfied with learning the proper proportions of ingredients and think that the work is done when the cooking begins. Food must be properly prepared, delicately seasoned, and served hot or cold as desired. Lukewarm, ill-seasoned food is unpalatable, and if served in a slovenly manner is most unappetizing. Any amount of seasoning at the table can not make up for poor seasoning in cooking. The same flavors can not be obtained. The only cook that should be styled a chef is one who uses the proper proportions in cooking, who delicately seasons his food and serves it in an appetizing manner.

The heat of cooking seems to create new flavors and to change the odor, taste, and digestibility of nearly all food. It swells and bursts the starch cells in flour, rice, and potatoes. It hardens the albumen of eggs, fish, and meat and softens the fibrous substances in tough meats, vegetables, and fruits. It develops new flavors in tea, coffee, roast meats, vegetables, crusts of bread, baked beans, etc.

Air (or the oxygen which it contains) plays an important part in the development of certain flavors. Steak broiled in the open air, bread toasted in the same manner, and roasted ears of corn possess certain flavors that can not be obtained in any other way.

It is also noticeable that articles of food cooked in a closed oven possess certain flavors that are lost if the cooking is done in the open air on the top of the range.

Baked apples have a particularly fine flavor, largely due to transformation of starch into sugar and to the caramelization of the sugar used in baking.

It is generally believed that certain vegetables, such as turnips and cabbages, should be well ventilated while boiling, in order that the obnoxious sulphurous and other gases may escape from the food and that, if this is not done, the vegetables will possess an inferior flavor, become discolored, and contain certain elements that are injurious. Nevertheless, cabbages and turnips can be boiled perfectly and will retain their fresh color and desirable flavor by submerging them in boiling water for a half hour or so, according to the size. In this way obnoxious fumes do not escape, but such sulphur as is extracted from the vegetables remains in the water.

Water is a necessity in certain forms of cooking. For example, beans and peas have to absorb a great deal of water to replace that lost in the process of ripening before they can be made into palatable food. The same may be said of desiccated (dried) fruits.

256. **Deep lard.**—The advantage of cooking in deep lard lies in the fact that lard or drippings can be heated to such an extremely high temperature that certain articles can be thoroughly cooked without giving time for the grease to soak into them. Grease boils at about 665 to 600° F., but this temperature is too high for cooking; the exterior of the food would be burned before it is cooked throughout.

The grease begins to smoke between 385 and 450° F., and this is the best temperature at which to use it. A common error is to introduce too much food at one time, cooling the fat and allowing it to soak into the food before it is thoroughly cooked. If this fact is borne in mind, almost anything that can be fried at all can be fried in "deep lard." Meat balls, potato balls, and croquettes are rolled in egg and cracker or bread crumbs before frying; the egg coagulates, and the crumbs, which are held in place by it, form a brown crust surrounding the ball, and the grease is prevented from penetrating further. Corn fritters contain eggs, and a good crust is quickly formed, preventing the penetration of the grease.

It is noticed that as soon as the articles mentioned have been dropped into the grease which is far below its boiling point a violent ebullition is observed. This is due to the escape of steam formed by contact of the moisture in the article introduced with the hot grease. All articles fried in deep lard should have as dry a surface as possible. If food with a damp surface is introduced, grease is apt to be thrown out upon the range, take fire, and cause trouble.

ELEMENTS OF NUTRITION.

257. The problem of proper nutrition has always been of great importance, yet scientific study of this subject is comparatively recent. Food investigation has been carried on in Europe for almost three-quarters of a century. It is more recent in the United States.

Constant use has made us familiar with our ordinary foods, but we seldom realize how complicated they are. To understand them requires much study of chemistry, physics, and physiology—more, indeed, than the average man desires to trouble with. However, we can better understand dieting and feeding of men by being familiar with a few of the elementary principles of nutrition.

258. The chemical composition of the body and of food are very similar. They are made up of the same chemical elements and should be discussed together. From 15 to 20 of these elements are found in both the body and food. The most abundant of these are oxygen, hydrogen, carbon, nitrogen, calcium, phosphorus, and sulphur. These elements are so combined as to form a great variety of compounds, of which the most important are protein, fats, carbohydrates, mineral matter, and water.

The functions of these compounds in the food are to build and repair the tissues, to furnish muscular and other power for the work the body has to do, and to furnish heat to keep the body warm.

259. **Water** is the most abundant of these compounds. It forms over 60 per cent of the weight of the body of the average man and is a component part of all the tissues. It is an important part of food, although it cannot be burned and yields no energy to the body.

200. **Mineral matter** yields little or no energy, yet is indispensable to the body. It forms only 5 or 6 per cent of the body by weight and is found chiefly

in the bones and teeth, but is also present in the other tissues and in solution in the various fluids. When food, or body material, is burned, the mineral constituents remain as ash.

261. **Protein.**—The term includes the principal nitrogenous compounds in foods which are the tissue formers and make the framework of the body, build up and repair the nitrogenous materials such as the muscles and tendons, and supply the albuminoids of the blood, milk, and other fluids.

These compounds form about 18 per cent of the weight of the body and are subdivided into:

Albuminoids, which include substances similar to the white of an egg, the lean of meat, curd of milk, and gluten of wheat.

Gelatinoids, which occur principally in the connective tissues, such as the collagen of the skin and tendons, and the ossein of the bones.

Extractives are the principal ingredients of meat extracts, beef tea, and beef stock. They are believed neither to build tissue nor to furnish energy, but to act as stimulants and appetizers. The craving, which some persons have for meats is believed to be due, in part, to a desire for these extractives. The same compounds are found in potatoes and other vegetable foods.

The *albuminoids* and *gelatinoids* are the most important elements of our food. They are essential, as they make the basis of bone, muscle, and other tissues. They are most abundant in animal food such as lean meat, though the cereals contain them to a considerable extent, and peas and beans in large proportion.

262. **Fats**, which form about 15 per cent of the weight of the ordinary man, occur chiefly in animal foods such as meat, fish, butter, etc. They are also abundant in some vegetable products such as olives and cotton seed, from which the oils are derived. They also are found in some cereals, notably oatmeal and maize and in various nuts. In our bodies, and those of other animals, fats occur in masses under the skin and in other locations and in minute particles throughout the tissues. The amount of fat in the body varies with conditions. When more food is taken than is necessary for immediate use part of it is stored as a reserve chiefly in the form of fat. When the food supply is short this reserve material is drawn upon for supplementary fuel.

263. **Carbohydrates**, which form only about 1 per cent of the body tissues, include such compounds as starches, sugars, and fibers of plants (cellulose). They are found chiefly in vegetable food—cereals, potatoes, and fruits—forming an abundant source of energy, and are important food ingredients,

easily digested. They are transformed into fat in the body and remain stored in concentrated form for future use.

264. **Refuse** is that part of our food, such as bones of fish and meat, shells of eggs, skins and seeds of fruit and vegetables, etc., which have little or no nutritive value and which are either unpalatable or can not be easily digested. These materials contain the same ingredients as the edible portions, though usually in smaller proportion.

265. **Use of expensive food.**—The mistake is often made of purchasing expensive varieties of food when cheaper ones will answer the purpose just as well. The cause of this error is ignorance of the simple principles of nutrition and the result is a waste of money. The maxim "the best is the cheapest" does not apply to the high-priced foods. The plain substantial standard food materials, like fish, milk, flour, corn meal, oatmeal, beans, potatoes, and the cheaper cuts of meat are as digestible and as nourishing to people in good health as the more expensive articles.

An understanding of the elements of nutrition, skillful cooking, and tasteful serving will effect a saving that will be surprising.

266. **A balanced diet** is one that supplies the proper amount of nourishment to the body without having any component greatly in excess of the requirements. Unless great care is exercised a diet will result which is one-sided or badly balanced; that is, one which gives an excess of either protein or carbohydrates. If a person eats large quantities of meat and few vegetables, the food is too rich in protein and probably harmful. On the other hand, if he eats vegetable food to the exclusion of meat he may overload his digestive organs with surplus food of that kind, which produces an excess of carbohydrates.

The Army ration, however, is well balanced and supplies the various ingredients in the proper proportions. The mess sergeant should study the following table of food values as a guide in purchasing the varieties of food required to make the mess attractive. He should endeavor to select the cheaper articles which assure the greatest fuel value, other things being equal,

267. The table is of special interest when comparing the usefulness to the system of different classes of foods or when determining the relative value of substitutive articles. For example, in order to keep down the expenses of a mess and to add variety it maybe desirable to substitute beans for meat on certain days. With either beans or meat, potatoes would probably be served, but when beans are placed on the bill of fare, they may take the place not only of meat, but also of a "second vegetable," as onions, tomatoes, cabbage, turnips, etc.

Assume that a mess of 100 men consumes at the noon meal 45 pounds of solid beef, and as a second vegetable, 25 pounds of onions.

From the tables of food values we note:

	Calories.
45 (pounds round) x 890 calories	40,050
25 (pounds onions) x 190 calories	4,750
Total	44,800

Now substitute a mess of beans for the above. Twenty-five rounds of beans and five pounds of bacon (for fat and flavor) are considered sufficient.

From the tables of food values we note:

	Calories.
25 (pounds beans) x 1,520 calories	38,000
5 (pounds bacon) x 2,715 calories	13,575
Total	51,575

Assuming that the latter are as fully digested as the meat and onions, it would seem that the ordinary addition of from 20 to 25 pounds of bacon is an unnecessary expense.

In the same way it may be shown that macaroni and cheese may be used as a satisfactory substitute for meat, and practical results bear out our theoretical deduction. In either case, the amount of protein (muscle-building material) and of fat and carbohydrates (energy producers) compare favorably with that found in the meat. In the same way it may be shown that fresh garden truck should not constitute the bulk of any meal.

Chapter V.

MANAGEMENT OF THE COMPANY MESS.

Kitchen economy.—In organizations of from 40 to 75 men the following enlisted men are required for duty in the company mess:

1 mess sergeant.
1 first cook.
1 second cook.
1 dining-room orderly.
2 cook's police.

For a larger organization, up to 115 men, there should be one additional cook's police. In organizations of from 115 to 150 men an additional cook should be provided.

Suggestions to mess sergeants.—The bills of fare should vary constantly. For each meal there should be at least one dish that has not been served for some time.

Seasonings penetrate foods best in the liquid or semiliquid state and much more quickly when hot than when cold, and consequently any amount of seasoning after the food is placed on the table can not compensate for insufficient or careless seasoning while in the course of preparation.

The prevention of waste and the proper use of left-over food is the secret of success in company kitchens.

The kitchen and storeroom should be kept scrupulously neat and the men required to clean up immediately after finishing each piece of work. Floors and tables should not be allowed to remain littered up after the necessity therefor has ceased. A piece of food left on the floor is sure to be stepped on, and will make dozens of spots instead of one. Cleanliness should be the first lesson taught.

The kitchen force should at all times present a neat, clean appearance. Especially should the cooks be clean as regards their toilet, as they are continually called upon to mix with their hands such articles as cakes, hashes, etc., and to handle nearly all food products in preparation for cooking. Men with dirty hands or untrimmed dirty fingernails communicate filth and disease germs to foodstuffs which they handle.

Each man should have definite duties assigned to him, for which he should be held solely responsible. Work must not be assigned in a general way to the kitchen force. If this is done, it frequently happens that some part of it is neglected and each man claims that he is not responsible.

No kitchen can be managed successfully unless each man knows what is expected of him. Should there be a failure on the part of anyone to perform his share of work, the responsibility should be fixed at once and punishment follow immediately.

Only those articles and cooking utensils being used in the kitchen or dining room should be kept by the mess sergeant. Other articles should be turned over to the supply sergeant so that they may be held in reserve to replace similar ones that may later become unserviceable. Moreover these surplus articles must be kept clean and this requires unnecessary labor.

Kitchens and adjoining rooms must be kept clean at all times. Such things as empty boxes and crates should not be allowed to accumulate. They litter up the storerooms and cellars and are very unsightly.

In cleaning shelves which are located in tiers, it is always best to commence with the topmost tier and work down. Otherwise the shelves underneath will be littered in cleaning those above.

The men should not spend all their time scouring the outside of boilers, pots, and pans. Let them spend some of that energy on the inside. The parts of the kitchen utensils which come in contact with the food are the most important and should receive the first and greatest attention. See to it that the inside of meat choppers and faucets on boilers are thoroughly cleaned, that the inside of bake pans, frying pans, boilers, and dish pans are well scoured, that the tines of forks and the junction of the blades and handles of knives and steels are clean—then attack the other parts. A kitchen may look very well to a superficial observer and still be extremely insanitary.

Each dish placed upon the table should be accompanied by a knife, fork, spoon, or ladle with which to serve the food contained therein. Men should not be allowed to serve themselves using their individual knives, forks, or spoons. Such a practice is not only disgusting but is a medium through which disease is transmitted from one person to another.

In cutting meat preparatory to serving, it should be held by a fork and not the hand, and after cutting, it should be transferred from the cutting board to the serving platters by the use of forks, skimmers, or other suitable utensils. The meat should never be handled with the hands. Frequently men put their hands in the lard in removing it from the tubs. This should not be permitted. Men who do such things are usually those who do not practice personal cleanliness and must be watched carefully in order to prevent them from transmitting disease to others.

Food that is liable to deteriorate should not be purchased in large quantities. In purchasing perishable articles, such as green onions, lettuce, radishes, etc., a supply for only one meal should be bought. Such vegetables are best when first picked.

Unless flour, corn meal, and other cereals can be kept in sealed metal containers, they should be purchased in lots sufficient only for three or four days. The accumulation of a large supply is apt to result in loss because of rats and mice. In summer fresh meat should be purchased in small quantities.

The warm weather of spring causes onions to sprout, particularly those that have been stored for some time. If not trimmed, these sprouts will sap the strength of the onion and render the vegetable useless. Cutting the sprouts helps to preserve onions. Furthermore the cut sprouts may advantageously be used in the kitchen in the preparation of soups, stews, hash, etc.

Whenever celery is served the tops should be cut off and used for seasoning. The cut tops may be placed in a paper bag and permitted to dry out. When dry they crumble like dead leaves but do not lose their strength for seasoning purposes.

Every effort should be made to keep flies out of the kitchen, dining room, and storerooms. They live and breed in places of filth where the germs of many diseases are most numerous. They light in germ-laden filth, a part of which clings to their feet and is carried away on them. The fly afterwards lights on the food and contaminates it with this filth and disease. In this way dysentery, diarrhea, typhoid fever, and other diseases are transmitted. Screening of doors and windows is absolutely necessary, and it is important to keep the screens closed whenever it is possible to do so and to keep the vicinity of the screen doors free from anything that attracts flies. Flies avoid dark places, and for that reason the dining room and kitchen should be kept darkened whenever it is convenient. When the police of the dining room is finished, it should be darkened.

All food in the kitchen and pantry should be kept covered whenever practicable, and all floors, tables, and table and kitchen ware should be cleaned after being used and should be kept free at all times possible from anything that attracts flies. Garbage stands should be kept whitewashed and the cans covered. The ground around the kitchen should be always so well policed that flies will not gather there.

Properly constructed flytraps are very effective in keeping down the flies. In camp they may be destroyed by burning out, with a torch after nightfall, the sides and roof of the kitchen tent. If the kitchen is darkened by drawing all the shades except one, which is kept raised about a foot, the flies gather on the lighted window sill and may be easily killed. A poison that kills flies but is harmless to man is made by placing in a shallow dish a solution of 2 ounces of water, a little sugar, and 1 dram of bichromate of potash.

It is important to kill the first flies of the season. One fly in May will probably have a peck of descendants by September; therefore he should be destroyed before he can commence to breed.

Rats, mice, and cockroaches are also carriers of disease and filth and destroyers of property. Like flies, they travel in filth and carry it on their feet to everything they touch. Unlike flies, they seek dark places where germs are most numerous. A good cat is the best protection against rats and mice. Cockroaches come out after dark and may be killed with a fly swatter, and also may be kept in check by means of roach powders sold on the market.

Considerable labor may be saved by the use of a piece of canvas 6 feet wide and from 10 to 14 feet long. After each meal has been served and the utensils emptied, the canvas is spread in front of the sink and all the utensils to be washed are placed thereon. Each utensil after being washed is returned to its proper place and the canvas taken up and hung out in the air. This not only protects the floor from sooty pots and boilers but also from grease that may fall from pans and from the sink.

Suggestions to cooks.—In order to work rapidly and spare himself unnecessary movements the cook should understand the recipe on which he is working. It is not necessary for him to remember all the recipes in the book. After the bill of fare is made out for the day he will save time and labor by sitting down, carefully reading it over, and getting into his head the necessary plan for all the details. There is nothing gained by starting work without a well-laid plan.

The cook should think of what he is going to do, remember how he did it before, and then try to do it a little better. He should observe how others do the same thing and, if possible, try to avoid all unnecessary movements in order to accomplish the most with the least possible work.

It is necessary to have a place for each utensil and to keep it there. Articles to be used, including most of the kitchen utensils and the food being prepared, should be placed within easy reach of the cook when standing in front of the kitchen range. In this way many unnecessary steps are saved.

When preparing cake much labor is saved by collecting all the necessary articles before beginning the mixing. Place these articles on the table at which the work is to be done, and before commencing work regulate the fire in the range. This is imperative for the reason that after getting the hands in the batter there is no time to collect articles and put coals on the fire. This applies also to all dishes prepared in the kitchen.

When getting ready to baste meat the cook often opens the oven door and pulls the pan out with a jerk, splashing some of the gravy in the oven and some on the floor. The door must then be scrubbed, and the grease which has fallen in the oven will burn and permeate the kitchen with a disagreeable odor and, in addition, the pans put in the stove thereafter will be soiled because of the unclean condition of the oven. More labor is used in cleaning the pans soiled by an unclean oven than is required to keep the oven clean.

Frequently a sooty boiler or pan is placed on the kitchen table or the draining board of a sink. A spot is left which must be removed at once. This may be avoided by the use of a board or rack on which sooty utensils can rest. Such a rack can easily be made by using five pine sticks ½ inch by 1 inch by 18 inches. Place two of them parallel to each other and about 14 inches apart. Across these nail the other three at intervals of about 6½ inches. Such a rack may be hung under the drain board of the sink when not wanted and, if needed, is immediately available.

When frying on the range, grease is often spilled upon the woodwork around the stove and on the kitchen floor. These grease spots should be removed at once by the use of plenty of hot water and soap. Not attending to this immediately results in spreading grease over the woodwork and more work in the end.

Spoons or other utensils used for stirring food should not be placed on the mantel of the range or the kitchen table. A plate should be placed on the table or mantel for the spoon to rest in. When a spoon or fork is taken from food on the stove a cloth should be held under it to catch the drippings.

In cutting meats good results can be obtained only by the use of sharp cutting utensils. Satisfactory and rapid work can not be accomplished with dull knives. The thumb should be held against the back of the knife, as this lessens the fatigue of the wrist and enables one to work more rapidly than if the thumb clasps the knife. Each kitchen should be provided with a good grindstone.

The plate and knife of the meat chopper should be kept closely together by means of the ring nut. If this is not done, particles of meat will edge in between the knife and plate and cause a ragged tearing of the meat. Often men loosen the ring nut with the idea that the handle can be more easily turned. Such is not the case, however, as the particles of meat torn off clog the chopper.

In trimming fat from meat no lean meat should be cut off with it. While rendering, the lean meat yields nothing but water and consequently becomes a total loss. In this regard it is better to allow some of the fat to remain on the meat, for during the cooking of the meat the drippings are caught in the pan and enrich the gravy prepared with the meat, or are skimmed from the stock in which the meat is boiled.

Gravy should be prepared in the pan in which the meat has been cooked. Some of the albuminous substances escape from the meat in the process of cooking and settle on the bottom of the pan. These add a flavor to the gravy that is not obtained if the drippings are drained into another pan and the gravy made in the latter. To the particles escaping from the meat should be added sufficient beef stock and flour to make a gravy of the proper consistency. During preparation, the gravy should be frequently stirred with a whip, in order to loosen the particles from the bottom of the pan. Where the meat cooked is very fat, excess drippings should be drained from the pan before the gravy is made.

If several pans are used for roasting, after the meat has been removed the drippings should be poured into one pan. Into the emptied pans should be poured either beef stock or hot water, which when brought to a boil and agitated with a wire whip will loosen the meat residue left on the bottom of the pans during roasting.

As a general rule food should be seasoned during the process of cooking. Cooks must be careful in the use of salt, especially in preparing hashes, meat balls, and stews from food that has been left over. The left-overs are from food which has previously been seasoned and, unless great care is taken, dishes subsequently prepared from them will be too salty. It must be borne in mind that it is better to put in too little salt than too much, because more may be added to the food in the dining room according to taste.

Buns and rolls for supper are usually baked by 1 p.m. They are then spread on tables to cool, a process that ordinarily does not require more than one hour. If they are left exposed until 5.30 or 6 p.m., they become hard and partly dried out. If, however, after being cooled, they are placed on their sides in a tightly closed boiler, they will remain soft and nutty, not only for supper but for the following breakfast. Not more than three tiers of buns or rolls should be placed in a boiler.

The following suggestions regarding the cooking of vegetables will be found useful:

(a) Cook green vegetables rapidly in boiling salt water, the time allowed depending on the vegetable cooked. All vegetables should be carefully drained after boiling.

(b) It is a good rule to use only enough water to cover the vegetables. If it evaporates, add more boiling water. Sulphurous vegetables, however, should be well immersed in water, otherwise they will be tough and discolored and their flavor changed.

(c) Vegetables are best when freshly gathered. If slightly wilted, soak them in cold water. Even when not wilted such soaking improves them, as it renders them more crisp and palatable. Onions, cabbages, and cauliflower, if soaked for one hour before cooking, are less objectionable in odor.

(d) Onions, cabbages, and cauliflower should be boiled in an uncovered pot and the water changed at least once while cooking. A pinch of soda may be added to the water.

(e) Beans and peas should be strung or shelled and washed quickly. If cold water is allowed to stand on them very long, it removes much of their nutritious quality.

(f) Care must be taken not to break the skins of beets, as much of the coloring matter will escape in cooking.

(g) Carrots should be scraped and turnips pared before cooking. Both should be sliced thin.

(h) After husking green corn all the silk should be removed from the ears. Corn should not be washed. It should be eaten the day it is pulled.

(i) Young potatoes should be scraped and old ones peeled. If boiled potatoes, after draining, are allowed to remain on the range a few minutes, with the lid off the boiler, their flavor will be much improved.

(j) Spinach should be thoroughly washed in several waters to insure the removal of the grit. After cooking, drain in a colander and dress with melted butter, pepper, and salt.

(k) Insects are likely to gather in the hearts of cabbages. If the heads are to be cooked whole, put them in the water head down to remove the insects.

(l) Small parsnips may be cooked whole; if large, they should be cut lengthwise. To keep the flesh from darkening, remove all specks and trim off the fine roots.

Serving the meal.—A meal, however well prepared, must be served properly to give satisfaction and to prevent unnecessary waste. This requires a system by which everything is brought on the table hot or cold, as intended. All of the tables must be served promptly and in an orderly manner. This requires every man of the kitchen detail to perform properly the particular duties assigned to him.

Five minutes before mess call the coffee (or other beverage), bread, and soup must be placed on the mess tables (the soup in 1-gallon tureens to tables of 10 men) and the salad and dessert on the bread table.

The dinner is now ready, and the mess sergeant goes into the dining room to superintend the service. The cooks remain in the kitchen and serve the food to the waiters as they come for it.

The food, after being cooked, must be arranged on clean platters, vegetable dishes, etc. The outside of these dishes must be kept clean and all drippings of sirup, gravy, etc., removed from them.

The table must be set with care and kept scrupulously neat. Order in the dining room and conduct at the table are influenced by the care with which arrangements are made for the reception of the men.

All the men at each table must finish their soup before the remainder of the meal is served at that table. The mess sergeant not only superintends the service, but personally assists and sees that all are served properly and without delay or confusion.

It often happens that while those at the first tables served are ready for dessert, those at the other tables are in the midst of the meal, or possibly still eating their soup. Constant supervision is therefore necessary to see that the service is prompt and orderly.

As the men finish at each table it is cleared off, the food left being transferred to other tables or returned to the kitchen, and the dishes placed in the sink for washing.

When all have finished their dinner the food still remaining on the serving trays is returned to the kitchen and the bill of fare is made out for supper, care being taken to use, if practicable, all the food left over from breakfast and dinner. At the same time the bills of fare are prepared for breakfast and dinner for the following day. The waste collected from the plates should not fill more than a quarter of an ordinary bucket. The men should be given all they will eat, but should not be permitted to take on their plates more than they are going to eat. Each man may help himself as often as he likes, but waste of food must be met with prompt punishment. After a few punishments there will be no further trouble. The men will see the benefit derived from careful management and economy and will appreciate the good results they themselves have helped to obtain.

૯૦

Opposite: US Army field mess, 1918.
(Harris and Ewing Collection, Library of Congress)

Chapter VIII.

RECIPES.

BREAKFAST DISHES.

Milk for breakfast foods (for 20 men).
>   2 1-pound cans evaporated milk.
>   8 ounces sugar

Add a pinch of salt and sufficient water to make 1 gallon. Whip well a few minutes.

Cakes, batter (for 60 men).
>   8 pounds flour.
>   2 pounds sugar.
>   16 eggs.
>   8 ounces baking powder.
>   1⅗ ounces salt.

Make a batter of the flour, sugar, salt, and eggs (if practicable, about 10 hours before the cakes are to be made). Just before cooking each portion of the batter, mix in the proper portion of baking powder and grease griddle. If for example, one-eighth of the above amount is to be baked at a time, 1 ounce of the baking powder should be added to each portion. Serve hot with butter, sirup, or both.

Cakes, buckwheat (for 60 men).
>   5 pounds buckwheat flour.
>   5 pounds wheat flour.
>   2½ pounds molasses, or
>   2½ pounds sugar.
>   2 ounces salt
>   10 ounces baking powder.

Mix the flour, salt, and molasses (or sugar), and add water to make a stiff batter. Just before cooking each portion of the batter add the baking powder and grease the pan, as explained in the preceding recipe. If desired, this batter may be set the evening before, with 3 cakes of dried yeast, allowing it to stand about 12 hours in a temperature of 80° F. In this case, 3 ounces of baking powder may be added, if desired, but this is not necessary. Serve hot with sirup, butter, or both.

Cakes, corn (for 60 men).
> 3 pounds flour.
> 3 pounds corn meal.
> 1½ pounds sugar.
> 12 eggs.
> 6 ounces baking powder.

Mix the flour, corn meal, sugar, and eggs into a batter, beating well for about five minutes, and let stand for 2 hours before using. Add the baking powder just before baking, mixing it into each portion, as explained for batter cakes. In no case should all of the baking powder be added at once. Serve hot with sirup, butter, or both.

Hot cakes.—In many organizations attempts to serve cakes have been given up on account of the apparent necessity of serving them cold. To obviate this, place a hot bake pan on the shelf in the range and as fast as the cakes are fried pile them carefully in tiers of about one dozen each and they will keep hot for a long time. Cover with a clean dish towel, and use one beneath the pile of cakes.

French toast (for 60 men).
> 17 pounds bread.
> 1 pound sugar.
> 1 pound sirup.
> 1 can evaporated milk,
> 1 quart water.
> 6 eggs.
> 2 pounds flour.

Cut the bread in slices about one-half inch thick; dip in a batter made of the eggs, flour, milk, sugar, and water; add salt to taste; fry the same as batter cakes. Serve hot with butter.

Hominy, fried (for 60 men).
>6 pounds hominy.
>4 gallons water.
>2 ounces salt.

Place the water in a boiler on the range; when boiling add the salt and hominy and boil 20 to 30 minutes; remove from the boiler, spread about 1 inch deep in well-greased pans, and allow to cool; cut in pieces about 2 inches square; roll in flour and fry in deep lard. Serve hot with sirup or butter.

Mush, corn meal (for 60 men).
>6 pounds corn meal.
>1½ pounds sugar, if not on table.
>1 ounce salt.
>4 gallons water.

Allow the water to come to a boil, add the salt (and sugar if not on table) and the corn meal, meanwhile whipping well to prevent lumping. Cook for about 20 minutes and then allow to stand about the same length of time where it will remain hot. Place in vegetable dishes and serve hot with fresh or evaporated milk poured over it.

Mush, corn meal, fried (for 60 men).
>7 pounds corn meal.
>4 gallons water.
>2 ounces salt.
>2 ounces sugar.

Prepare in the same manner as corn meal mush; pour into a well-greased bake pan to a depth of about 1 inch; allow to cool; cut into pieces about 2 inches square; roll in a flour batter; and fry in deep lard. Serve hot with sirup.

This preparation may be improved by dipping each piece in an egg batter before rolling in the flour.

SOUPS

Barley and tomato soup (for 60 men).

5½ gallons beef stock.

3 pounds barley.

10 pounds tomatoes.

1 pound diced bacon.

Mix all ingredients well, salt and pepper to taste, and allow to boil for one hour. If fresh tomatoes are used they should be stewed and pressed through a colander before being added to the soup. Regulate the amount of beef stock so that when the soup is ready to serve there will be about 6 gallons.

Beef soup (for 60 men).

6 gallons beef stock.

3 pounds beef.

1 can tomatoes.

1½ pounds rice, if desired.

1 bunch parsley, if desired.

This soup may be made to best advantage on days when boiled beef is served. After boiling the beef until done take it out and skim off the grease; dice the beef to the size of a bean and add the water (or stock); add the tomatoes and, if desired, a little rice; regulate the amount of beef stock so that when the soup is ready to be served there will be about 6 gallons. Season to taste and serve hot.

Chicken soup (for 60 men).

6 gallons beef stock.

10 pounds chicken.

1 pound rice.

4 ounces parsley.

After dressing boil the chicken until well done; remove it and take out the bones; place the bones in the beef stock and boil for one hour; remove the bones and strain the stock; dice the chicken very fine and place in a boiler with the beef stock, add the rice, and boil for one-half hour; add enough stock and water to make 6 gallons; pepper and salt to taste. Before serving place a little parsley in each tureen.

Clam chowder (for 60 men).

 6 quarts clams.

 8 pounds potatoes, diced.

 1 pound bacon, diced and browned.

 10 quarts beef stock.

 ½ pound chopped onions, browned.

Cook the potatoes, bacon, and onions in the beef stock until well done, add the clams, and let come to a boil; thicken slightly with a flour batter and it will be ready to serve. Salt and pepper to taste and regulate the amount of beef stock so that when the soup is ready to serve there will be about 6 gallons.

Codfish chowder (for 60 men).

 5 pounds codfish, shredded.

 1½ pounds bacon, diced.

 1½ pounds onions, chopped.

 6 pounds potatoes, diced.

 1 pound hard bread.

 2 cans evaporated milk, if desired.

 6 gallons beef stock.

Brown the bacon and onions in a bake pan on the top of the range; add the potatoes and codfish and cover well with stock; boil until done, about 20 minutes; break the hard bread in small pieces and toast slightly in the oven, adding to the chowder after the potatoes are done. Then add the milk, if it is desired, and season to taste. Regulate the amount of beef stock so that when the soup is ready to serve there will be about 6 gallons.

Corn chowder (for 60 men).

 3 No. 2 cans corn.

 1½ pounds diced bacon.

 1½ pounds onions.

 6 pounds potatoes, diced.

 4 gallons beef stock.

 2 cans evaporated milk.

 1 pound hard bread.

Fry the bacon and onions in a bake pan on top of the range until brown; add the potatoes and cover with stock; boil until done; break up the hard bread into small pieces; toast slightly and add to the chowder when the potatoes are done; add the milk and corn, but do not allow to boil; season to taste. Regulate the amount of beef stock so that when the soup is ready to serve there will be about 6 gallons.

Cream of cabbage (for 60 men).

    6 pounds cabbage, chopped fine.

    6 gallons beef stock.

    2 1-pound cans evaporated milk.

    1 pound fat, butter preferred.

    1 pound flour, browned in the fat.

Boil the cabbage about 15 minutes; drain the water off and add the beef stock; cook about one hour; thicken with a flour batter, and just before serving season with white pepper, salt, and celery salt, and add the milk. Emulate the amount of beef stock so that when the soup is ready to serve there will be about 6 gallons.

Cream of celery (for 60 men).

    6 pounds celery, diced fine.

    5 gallons beef stock.

    1 pound fat, butter preferred.

    1 pound flour, browned in fat.

    2 1-pound cans evaporated milk.

Add the celery to the beef stock and boil about one hour; season with white pepper, celery salt, and salt; thicken with batter made of the fat and flour, and just before serving add the milk. Regulate the amount of beef stock so that when the soup is ready to serve there will be about 6 gallons.

Macaroni soup (for 60 men).

    3 pounds macaroni.

    6 gallons beef stock.

    ½ pound chopped onions, browned if desired.

    1 pound bacon, browned if desired.

Break the macaroni in pieces about 1 inch long and boil in the stock about, 40 minutes, seasoning to taste with salt and pepper. Regulate the amount of beef stock so that when the soup is served there will be about 6 gallons.

Noodle soup (for 60 men). Prepared the same as macaroni soup, using 4 pounds dry noodles instead of 3 pounds macaroni.

To prepare the noodles.—To each pound of flour add one-fifth ounce of salt; mix with milk and water until the dough is stiff. If practicable, add two eggs to each pound of flour used. Roll the dough out until it is about one-eighth of an inch thick; sprinkle a little flour over it and roll it up. Cut slices from the end of the roll about one-eighth to one-fourth inch thick and spread on a board or cloth in the sun to dry. The noodles thus prepared will keep indefinitely.

Oxtail soup (for 60 men).
    8 pounds oxtail, chopped into one-half inch cubes.
    5 gallons beef stock.
    2 pounds fried carrots, diced.
    2 pounds fried onions, diced.
    2 No. 3 cans tomatoes.
    1 pound fat, butter preferred.
    1 pound flour, browned in fat.

Add the oxtail, carrots, onions, and tomatoes to the beef stock, and let simmer until the tails are well done; thicken with the flour batter. Regulate the amount of beef stock so that when the soup is ready to be served there will be about 6 gallons. The above recipe should produce a thick soup of a reddish color. Serve hot.

Oyster stew (for 60 men).
    12 No. 2 cans oysters.
    5 gallons beef stock.
    3 1-pound cans evaporated milk.
    ½ bottle Worcestershire sauce.

Drain off the liquor; thicken the beef stock slightly with the flour batter, and add the liquor from the oysters; bring to a boil; season to taste with salt, pepper and Worcestershire sauce, and boil five minutes. Regulate the amount of beef stock so that when the stew is ready to serve there will be about 6 gallons. Add the oysters just before serving,

Pea soup (for 60 men).

> 6 No. 2 cans green peas, or equivalent of fresh peas.
>
> 6 gallons beef stock.

Allow to boil 10 minutes if canned peas are used, or until well done in the case of fresh peas. Regulate the amount of beef stock so that when the soup is ready to serve there will be about 6 gallons.

Potato soup (for 60 men).

> 10 pounds potatoes, diced.
>
> 6 gallons beef stock.
>
> 1 pound onions, chopped and browned.
>
> 1 can evaporated milk.
>
> 1 pound fat, butter preferred.
>
> 1 pound flour, browned in fat.

Boil the potatoes in the stock until well done; pass through a colander and let come to a boil again; thicken with the flour batter and season to taste; add the chopped onions and evaporated milk. Regulate the amount of beef stock so that when the soup is ready to serve there will be about 6 gallons. Serve hot.

Purée of beans (for 60 men).

> 6 pounds issue beans.
>
> 6 gallons beef stock.
>
> 5 pounds soup bone.
>
> ½ pound bacon, diced and browned.
>
> 1 pound fat, butter preferred.
>
> 1 pound flour, browned in fat.

Place the beans, bacon, bone, and stock in the boiler, and let simmer over night, or until the beans are thoroughly broken to pieces. Pass through a colander, and place on the stove again; add the flour batter and season to taste; allow to simmer at least one hour before serving. Regulate the amount of beef stock so that, when the soup is ready to serve, there will be about 6 gallons.

Purée of potatoes (for 60 men).

    12 pounds potatoes, diced fine.

    6 gallons beef stock.

    1 pound bacon, diced and browned.

    1 pound fat, butter preferred.

    1 pound flour browned in fat.

Add the diced potatoes and bacon to the beef stock and boil until they are completely broken to pieces, seasoning with pepper, salt, and celery salt, etc. A stalk of celery may be added if desired. Thicken slightly with the flour batter, when it will be ready to serve. Regulate the amount of beef stock so that, when the soup is ready to serve, there will be about 6 gallons.

Rice soup (for 60 men).

    3 pounds rice.

    6 gallons beef stock.

    ½ pound chopped onions, browned.

    1 pound bacon, diced and browned.

Wash the rice well; then add it, together with the bacon and onions, to the stock, and allow to boil for one-half hour.

Rivel soup (for 60 men).

    3 pounds flour.

    6 eggs.

    6 gallons beef stock.

Rub the eggs and flour together in the hands until well mixed; then add the rivels thus made to the stock and allow to boil for one-quarter of an hour. Season with pepper and salt. One can of tomatoes may be added if desired.

Split-pea soup (for 60 men).

    6 pounds split peas.

    6 gallons beef stock.

    1 pound flour.

    1 pound bacon, diced and browned.

Add the peas and the bacon to the beef stock and let simmer over night, thicken with a flour batter; season to taste and serve hot. Regulate the amount of beef stock so that, when the soup is ready to serve, there will be about 6 gallons.

Tomato soup (for 60 men).
>   3 gallons tomatoes, or
>   8 No. 3 cans tomatoes.
>   3 gallons beef stock.
>   1 pound bacon.

Mix all the ingredients well and boil for one and one-half hours; remove the bacon and press the soup through a colander to separate the skins and seeds or the tomatoes. Replace on the range and thicken slightly with a flour batter; salt and pepper to taste, and color lightly with brown sugar. Regulate the amount of beef stock so that, when the soup is ready to serve, there will be about 6 gallons.

Overripe or bruised tomatoes may, to prevent waste, be used in the preparation of this soup.

Vegetable soup (for 60 men).
>   1 pound cabbage.
>   ½ pound onions.
>   1 pound potatoes,
>   ½ pound rice.
>   1 can tomatoes.
>   1 ounce chopped parsley.
>   5 gallons beef stock.

Mix all ingredients well; season to taste with salt and pepper; boil for one hour or more, when it will be ready to serve. Regulate the amount of beef stock so that, when the soup is ready to serve, there will be about 6 gallons. The parsley should generally be added just before serving. Many other vegetables may be substituted for those given above.

Welsh rarebit (for 60 men).
>   6 gallons beer, or beef stock.
>   6 pounds grated cheese, American preferred.
>   1½ pounds fat, butter preferred.
>   1½ pounds flour, browned in fat.

Allow the beer or stock to come to a boil, and add the grated cheese. Make a batter of the butter and flour, and, when smoking hot, add to the mixture. Season with salt and cayenne pepper. Serve in soup tureens with crackers or croutons.

MEATS.

Bacon and cabbage (for 60 men).

    15 pounds bacon, sliced.
    30 pounds cabbage.

Wash and clean the cabbage; place in the boiler with sufficient water to cover it; place bacon on top of the cabbage; boil two hours. To prevent discoloration, the boiler should be ventilated during the process of cooking. Serve hot with the bacon on top of the cabbage.

Beef à la mode (for 60 men).

    20 pounds beef rounds, bottom preferred
    1 pound bacon or pork.
    1 pound fat, butter preferred.
    1 pound flour, browned in fat.
    3 gallons beef stock.
    1 pound carrots, diced.
    4 large issue pickles.
    2 cans tomatoes.

Cut the beef into slices of about 5 pounds each and the bacon (or pork) into strips about the size of the little finger and the length of the pieces of beef; roll the strips of pork in garlic and cayenne pepper and cut slits in the pieces of beef with a narrow-bladed knife with the grain of the meat, and insert about four of these strips of bacon with slices of pickle in each piece of beef. Make a gravy of the flour, fat, and beef stock; place in a medium-hot oven and cook slowly for about three hours, or until well done. Remove the meat and slice across the grain, replace in the gravy, and cook a little longer; or slice and place on a platter with the gravy poured over it, in which case it is ready to serve. It should be served with hot gravy. The gravy should be very spicy; therefore, while preparing it season well with garlic, bay leaves, etc.

Beef, corned (for 60 men).

    4 gallons water.
    2 pounds sugar.
    8 ounces saltpeter.
    16 ounces salt.
    60 pounds beef.

Dissolve and boil about 15 minutes; pour into a 15-gallon keg and allow to cool. The brine should be prepared in the evening so that it will be given time to cool thoroughly before the meat is introduced. Cut the meat in pieces weighing about 5 pounds each and probe each piece with a steel at 1-inch intervals to allow the brine to penetrate all parts. Place the meat in the brine and keep at a temperature of from 50° to 60° F. from seven to nine days. While in the brine it should be removed at least three times, alternating the upper and lower pieces. If the beef used is not refrigerated beef, in hot weather it should be packed in cracked ice for 12 hours before corning. The above recipe is sufficient for corning 60 pounds.

To make spiced corned beef, place in the center of each piece of beef a small piece of garlic, and add to the brine 1 ounce each of cloves, whole peppers, and bay leaves.   ·

To cook, use the recipe for boiled beef.

Beef, curry (for 60 men).
    20 pounds beef.
    ½ ounces curry powder.
Cut the beef into 1-inch cubes and place in a bake pan; cover with beef stock or water; season with salt, pepper, and curry powder. When nearly done, thicken slightly with a flour batter. Serve hot.

Beef dressing (for 60 men).
    6 pounds meat scraps of any kind.
    8 pounds bread.
    1 pound onions, browned.
    1½ gallon beef stock.
Run the meat scraps through a chopper; soak the bread in cold water and squeeze well with the hands; mix the meat and bread with the onions; season with salt, pepper, and sage, add sufficient beef stock to make about the same consistency as hash; and spread 2 or 3 inches deep over the bottom of a well-greased pan. Spread a little grease over the top and bake for 40 minutes in a medium oven. Serve hot with beef and gravy.

Beef, chipped (for 60 men).

    15 pounds chipped beef.
    1 pound fat, butter preferred.
    1¼ pounds flour, browned in fat.
    2 cans evaporated milk.
    1 bunch parsley.
    ¼ ounce pepper.
    6 quarts beef stock.

Melt the fat in the pan and add the flour; cook a few minutes; mix the milk and beef stock, or water; stir the batter in slowly to prevent lumping; add the beef and cook a few minutes. Add the parsley and serve on toast.

If the beef is very salty, it should be scalded before cooking.

Beef fritters (for 60 men).

    10 pounds cooked beef.
    5 pounds bread.
    2 pounds onions.

Soak the bread and remove the water by squeezing with the hands; grind the meat fine and add to the bread; mince the onions and mix all together; salt and pepper to taste; mold into cakes of about 3 ounces each; roll in flour and fry in deep grease until brown.

Serve hot with tomato sauce or tomato gravy.

Beef hash (for 60 men).

    15 pounds potatoes.
    2 pounds onions.
    15 pounds meat scraps, etc.
    6 quarts beef stock.

Chop the whole fine and add the beef stock until the mixture is of the consistency of ordinary mush; place about 3 inches deep in a well-greased pan; smooth the top evenly with the hand and grease slightly; bake in a quick oven for 1½ hours, or until done.

Scraps of beef or pork, or a mixture of both, or corned beef may be used for making hash.

In hot weather, or when the ingredients have been held over for some time, the hash should be spread not more than 2 inches deep in a pan and first placed in a quick oven, about 10 counts, until the hash is thoroughly heated through, about 20 minutes; then the temperature may be reduced until the cooking is done.

Beef hash with green peppers. Prepare in the same manner as beef hash, adding 2 or 3 pounds of green peppers chopped about the size of a Lima bean.

Beef hearts, stuffed (for 60 men).
>   18 pounds beef hearts.
>   6 pounds bread crumbs.
>   2 pounds onions, browned.
>   1 pound bacon, sliced.
>   ¼ pound fat.

Wash and clean the hearts and allow to drain; soak the bread crumbs, squeeze out well, and mix with the fried onions. Season the mixture with thyme, pepper, and salt, and stuff the holes in the hearts with this dressing. Place the hearts in a bake pan with a slice of bacon on top of each, and bake in a moderately hot oven. After the hearts have become somewhat sealed, so as to retain the juices, the temperature of the oven should be gradually reduced. Before serving, place the dressing on a platter, slice the hearts thin, and spread over the dressing.

Beef loaf (for 60 men).
>   12 pounds beef.
>   3 pounds bread crumbs.
>   2 pounds onions, browned.
>   1 pound flour.
>   1 or 2 quarts beef stock,
>   ½ pound bacon.

Grind the meat through a chopper; soak the bread in water and then squeeze out well; mix the meat, bread crumbs, and onions together; season with salt and pepper; make into loaves about the shape of an egg divided lengthwise and place in a bake pan a few inches apart. Then make a batter of the flour and beef stock, rub this over the loaves, and cook in a slow oven. A slice of bacon may be placed on the top of each loaf, if desired, and serve hot with gravy.

Beef potpie (for 60 men).

> 15 pounds beef.
>
> 15 pounds potatoes.
>
> 3 pounds onions.
>
> 2 pounds lard,
>
> 5 pounds flour.

Cut the beef into 1-inch cubes; stew until nearly done; add potatoes and onions, cut into about 1-inch cubes. When nearly done, pepper and salt to taste and add sufficient stock to cover vegetables and meat and thicken slightly with flour batter. When done, cover with crust made of the lard, flour, and baking powder, cut out like biscuits, and bake until done. The amount of beef may be reduced to 10 pounds and vegetables increased accordingly.

Any kind of lean meat—mutton, veal, venison, young goat, chicken, wild fowls, and rabbits—may be used in making potpies.

Beef, roast (for 60 men).

> 25 pounds beef.
>
> 1 quart beef stock.

Cut the beef into pieces weighing about 5 pounds each; place in a quick oven and cook for about one-half hour; then dredge with salt, pepper and flour, and add 1 quart of beef stock, adding more later if necessary. The roast will then be sealed so as to retain the juices and the temperature of the oven should be allowed to diminish gradually, cooking the meat slowly from one to two hours more. Baste frequently while roasting. Just before serving, cut into thin slices, across the grain, and retain all chunks of fat, bones, tendons, etc., as they will not be consumed if served, but can be used to great advantage in the kitchen. Serve hot with gravy.

Yorkshire pudding (for 60 men). Roast the beef in the usual, way. When it is done pour off and save half the juice, which is used in making gravy.

> 6 pounds flour.
>
> 5 ounces baking powder.
>
> 1 ounce salt.
>
> Pinch of cayenne pepper.

Mix all ingredients dry; add sufficient flour and water to make a dough somewhat softer than used for biscuits. Drop the dough from the hand into the pan in which the beef was roasted, keeping each handful about 1 inch apart. Bake in a medium oven. The above recipe will be improved by adding two to six eggs to each pound of flour used; whip eggs to foam, and mix in well. By substituting milk for water the product is greatly improved.

Beef rolls (for 60 men).
>   8 pounds meat scraps, etc.
>   3 pounds bread crumbs.
>   5 pounds flour.
>   1 pound onions, browned.
>   1 ounce chili pepper.

Pass the meat scraps through a chopper; soak the bread crumbs and squeeze well; mix well the meat, bread, and seasoning of salt, onions, chili pepper, etc. Make a pie crust or rich biscuit dough and roll into long strips as for apple rolls. Spread the meat and bread mixture over the dough; roll up in lengths equal to that of the bake pan; garnish the top with beaten eggs; and bake in a slow oven.

Beef, Spanish (for 60 men).
>   20 pounds beef.
>   2 No. 3 cans tomatoes.
>   5 pounds onions, chopped.

Cut the beef into 1½ inch cubes; fry in a little hot fat for about five minutes; pour off the fat and add the tomatoes and onions. Add sufficient beef stock to cover the meat; thicken with a flour batter; season with salt and pepper, and allow to simmer for two hours. Serve hot.

Scraps of cooked meat may be used to the extent of one-half of the meat component, in which case it should be allowed to cook for but one-half hour.

Beefsteak and mushrooms (for 60 men).
>   20 pounds beefsteak, without bones or fat.
>   6 No. 2 cans mushrooms.
>   1 pound butter.
>   1 pound flour.

Prepare the beefsteak in the ordinary manner; place the butter in a frying pan; when smoking hot, pour the flour into the pan and stir well to prevent it from burning. After it becomes smooth pour in the liquor from the mushrooms, beating well with a wire whipper; add the diced mushrooms and boil for five minutes. Place the fried steak on the platter and pour the mushrooms and gravy over the steak. Serve hot.

Beefsteak, Hamburg (for 60 men).
>20 pounds beef.
>3 pounds onions.

Run the meat through a chopper twice; chop the onions fine with knives; mix well and season with pepper and salt; mold into steaks about 3 inches in diameter and about one-half inch in thickness; roll in flour and fry in deep lard. Serve hot with gravy.

Beef, Turkish (for 60 men).
>18 pounds beef.
>5 pounds rice.
>1 pound fat, butter preferred.
>1 pound flour, browned in fat.
>2 pounds onions, browned.
>3 gallons stock.

Make a batter of the flour and fat, adding the stock and onions to make a gravy. Cut the meat in 1-inch cubes; season with cayenne pepper, salt, and a little garlic; roll in flour and fry in deep lard. After the meat is fried, put immediately in the gravy and allow to simmer for two hours. While cooking it may be necessary to add a little more stock. Meanwhile boil the rice (and fry if desired) and place around the platter, making a nest in the center into which the stew is poured.

Brains and eggs (for 60 men).
>15 pounds beef brains.
>2 pounds bacon.
>2 pounds onions, chopped fine.
>40 eggs.
>2 ounces salt.
>½ ounce pepper.

Clean and wash the brains well and dice into about one-half inch cubes; dice the bacon into small cubes or run it through a meat chopper; fry the bacon and onions until brown; add the brains and cook until nearly done (about three-quarters of an hour); add the eggs, beaten slightly, and fry about 10 minutes more. Season with salt and pepper. Serve on platters covered with small bits of dipped or dry toast, if desired.

This preparation may be enriched by the addition of more eggs reducing the amount of brains in proportion.

Chicken, curry of (for 60 men).

    25 pounds chicken.

    1½ ounces curry powder.

    6 pounds rice.

    1 quart flour (if desired for batter).

Cut each chicken into about 10 or 12 pieces; wash well and place in a large bake pan, covering with about 3 inches of water. When it reaches the boiling point, allow to simmer two hours or until done. Season to taste with salt after the chicken has cooked about an hour. Meanwhile make a paste of the curry powder and about a quart of broth from the pan, add to the chicken and when served garnish the platter with boiled rice. If desired, the mixture may be thickened by the addition of a flour batter.

Chicken fricassee (for 60 men).

    25 pounds chicken.

    2 pounds butter.

    1 pound flour.

    1 stalk celery.

    12 hard-boiled eggs.

    2 cans evaporated milk.

    3 gallons beef stock.

Divide each chicken into about 12 pieces, natural divisions. Make a gravy, using 1 pound butter, 1 pound flour, and the beef stock. Pepper and salt the chicken well; roll in flour and fry in deep lard; and put it in the gravy when fried. Dice the celery and add to the gravy; season well with celery salt and allow to simmer until done, before serving add 2 cans of evaporated milk and 1 pound of butter. Care should be taken to break up the chicken as little as possible. When adding the butter and milk, have the gravy so thick that the butter will be taken up by it and not float on top. Serve on a platter, with or without rice. Old fowls may be utilized to good advantage in this recipe.

Chicken, fried (for 60 men).

> 45 pounds chicken.
>
> 6 eggs, beaten.
>
> 2 pounds cracker meal.

Fowls over 6 months old should not be fried. Divide each chicken into about 10 pieces; dip each piece in the beaten eggs and then in the cracker dust, and if the mixture does not adhere to the pieces sufficiently, repeat the operation. Fry in deep lard at a smoking temperature until brown. Drain well in a colander and place in a pan in the oven or on the mantel of the range to keep warm until served.

Chicken, roast (for 60 men).

> 45 pounds chicken.
>
> 2 pounds minced onions, browned.
>
> 8 pounds bread crumbs.
>
> 8 pounds potatoes, mashed.
>
> 1 pound flour.
>
> 1 pound fat, butter preferred.

Pick and clean chicken well, saving the heart, liver, and gizzard which should be chopped fine and used in the gravy or stuffing. Fill space vacated by entrails and craw with stuffing. Sew up chicken with strong thread and bend the wings under the back and tie down to the body. Make a batter with the flour and fat, seasoning it with salt and pepper, and rub the chicken with it before placing in oven. After the chicken has been in the oven about 20 minutes, add a little hot water and baste frequently until done. This generally requires about two and one-half hours, depending upon the quality of the fowl. When the flour is brown check the heat. When done the legs can be easily separated from the body.

To make the stuffing.—Moisten the bread crumbs with water; mix with potatoes, onions, and giblets; season with pepper and salt, sage, thyme, or other flavors; stuff well into the chicken. The bread may be soaked in oyster liquor and oysters added to the stuffing; or celery, currants, or raisins may be used instead of onions. Lemon juice or nuts may be added. This stuffing may be used with any fowl or fish.

Chicken stew with dumplings (for 60 men).

    25 pounds chicken.

    15 pounds potatoes, diced.

    5 pounds flour for dumplings.

Cut each chicken into 10 or 12 pieces and place in sufficient hot water to cover it; boil until nearly done. Then thicken the stew slightly with a flour batter; season with salt and pepper; add dough for the dumplings and allow to cook 10 or 15 minutes, depending on the size of the dumplings. If desired, the amount of dumplings, may be increased and the amount of chicken correspondingly reduced. Time to prepare, about two and one-half hours.

Chili con carne (for 60 men).

    15 pounds meat scraps.

    3½ ounces chili peppers, ground.

    3½ quarts beans, chili.

Trim all the fat from the meat and chop into half-inch cubes; place in a bake pan and fry in the same manner as beefsteak, but using a smaller amount of fat; cover with about 1 inch of beef stock; add the ground chili pepper and salt to taste. Run two-thirds of boiled chili beans through a meat chopper and mix all together; then add the remaining third of the beans whole. While cooking it may be necessary to add more beef stock to replace that lost by evaporation. When ready to serve, there should be sufficient beef stock to cover the preparation. Baked beans may be substituted for chili beans.

Head cheese (for 60 men).

    20 pounds beef.

    10 pounds pork.

Use any kind of beef scraps; of the pork, use snout, ears, skin, feet, etc. Place in separate pots and boil. When the pork is done, remove and pass through a meat chopper, allowing the beef to continue boiling until well done. Remove the beef and dice in one-half inch cubes; mix the whole and season with pepper, salt, vinegar, and cloves, adding sufficient stock in which the meat was cooked to give it the consistency of a thick stew. Replace on the range, boil five minutes longer, and pour in a pan about 4 inches deep; cool in a temperature of 50° to 60° F., and it will be ready to serve the next day.

Liver and bacon in gravy (for 60 men).

 15 pounds liver.
 8 pounds bacon.
 6 pounds onions, browned.
 2 pounds flour.
 4 gallons stock.

Slice the bacon thin and wash in boiling hot water, not allowing it to remain in the water more than five minutes; fry quickly until medium well done. Roll the slices of liver in flour and fry in the fat left after frying the bacon; add the liver and bacon to the stock and bring to a boil; thicken slightly with a flour batter; add the onions and salt to taste. Serve hot.

Mutton stew (for 60 men).

 15 pounds mutton.
 20 pounds potatoes.
 4 pounds onions.

Cut the mutton into 1-inch cubes; add sufficient beef stock or cold water to just cover the mutton; allow to simmer slowly for one and one-half hours, or until the mutton is done; add the vegetables, and cook until done; season to taste with pepper and salt, and thicken slightly with a flour batter. Serve hot, with or without dumplings.

Omelet (for 60 men).

 120 eggs.
 4 cans evaporated milk.
 1 pound drippings.

Mix the eggs and evaporated milk; pepper and salt to taste; add 1 quart of water and whip well; put 1 pound of bacon drippings or other fat into the bake pan, and when the fat begins to smoke pour in the mixture (not more than 3 inches deep) and bake in a medium oven.

Cheese omelet.—Add to the mixture before cooking about 3 pounds of diced cheese.

Ham omelet.—Add to the mixture before cooking about 3 pounds of finely chopped cooked ham.

Tomato omelet.—Prepare in the same manner as the plain omelet, substituting two small cans of tomatoes for the water.

Army cooks learning their trade at the Pratt Institute, Brooklyn, New York, August 1917. (George Grantham Bain Collection, Library of Congress)

Pigs, little, roasted (for 60 men).

    40 pounds little pigs.

    Clean the pigs and scrape off the hair, stuff with an ordinary dressing, and sew up. Slit the throat, and pass the forelegs through to the front; double the hind legs under, the pig lying down on its stomach. Season well on the outside. If practicable, place in a pan so that no part of the pig projects above the top. Pour into the pan about 1 inch of beef stock. Roll out a dough made of water and flour and spread over the pig, moistening the sides of the pan with water so that the crust will adhere to it. Bake slowly three or four hours.

Pickled pigsfeet (for 60 men).

    25 pounds pigsfeet.

These are purchased ready to serve cold and are well liked if not served too often. They may be rolled in batter and fried to a golden brown.

Pork, corned, with cabbage (for 60 men);

    20 pounds corned pork.

    25 pounds cabbage.

Wash and clean the cabbage; place in a boiler with sufficient water to cover the cabbage; place about one-third of the pork on top of the cabbage, cooking the remainder in a separate boiler. Allow all to simmer about two hours. To prevent discoloration, the boiler should be ventilated during the process of cooking. Serve hot, the pork being sliced and placed on top of the cabbage.

Pudding, English beef (for 60 men).

    12 pounds beef.

    8 pounds flour.

    8 ounces baking powder.

    1 pound lard.

    2 ounces salt.

Run the meat through the chopper twice. Season with salt, pepper, and two cloves of garlic. Braise in fat. Make a dough somewhat stiffer than a biscuit dough, with the flour, baking powder, lard, and salt. Roll out the dough one-fourth inch thick and 20 inches wide; spread meat over the top about the same thickness as the dough. Roll up the meat in the dough as though it were a jelly roll, rolling a little tighter. Have six duff cans well greased and cut the roll in such lengths as to fill the cans about three-fourths full. Steam, same as plum duff, from five to six hours. After the cans are removed from the boiler allow them to stand about 10 minutes before emptying. Serve with brown or onion gravy.

Sausage, bologna, with casings removed (for 60 men).

    20 pounds bologna sausage.

Slice about 1 inch thick; dip in batter and fry in deep lard; serve hot; or slice an inch thick; braise with onions in the oven; serve hot. It may also be served cold with salad or made into sandwiches. It is cheaper than beef and will be relished if prepared not oftener than once a week.

Sausage, liver, with casings removed (for 60 men).

   20 pounds liver sausage.

This generally comes in small casings. If in this form cut about 2 inches in length, remove casings, dip in egg batter, roll in crumbs or cracker dust, then fry in deep lard. When supplied in large casings it is better to cut it in half-inch slices, and prepare in the same manner. It may be served with a salad, or bologna, for sandwiches. Blood sausage may be prepared and served in the same manner.

Sausage pork, 65-pound mixture.

   40 pounds pork.
   25 pounds beef.
   1½ pounds salt.
   6 ounces black pepper.
   1 ounce coriander.
   1½ ounce sage.
   1 pint vinegar.
   1 clove garlic.

Dice the pork in 1½-inch squares. Grind the beef and mix with the pork, add seasoning and mix well; then grind again. The more thoroughly the sausage is mixed the better it will be.

This should stand three days in a temperature under 60° F. before being used.

Sausage, pork, in blankets (for 60 men).

   20 pounds link sausages.
   1 egg beaten.
   1 pound lard.
   3 pounds flour.
   1 ounce salt.

Make a dough of the three last-named articles and roll out as for pie crust; inclose each link separately, or two links in one piece of dough; garnish with the egg and a little water and bake until a delicate brown.

Stew, el rancho (for 60 men).

    12 pounds meat, fresh, without bone and but little fat, cut in about 1½-inch cubes.

    10 pounds potatoes.

    2 cans tomatoes, or

    6 pounds fresh tomatoes.

    3 pounds carrots, quartered lengthwise.

    4 pounds turnips, sliced across grain.

    4 pounds cabbage, with core in cabbage. Cut from top to bottom, in quarters or eighths, depending on size of head.

    3 pounds onions, small preferred, whole.

Place the meat and such vegetables as turnips, carrots, and tomatoes in a large pan of cold water and bring slowly to a boil. Let simmer until the meat is tender and then add the remaining vegetables, season with salt, chili colorado, comina, and oregano, and cook until done. All ingredients should be thoroughly cooked but not broken into pieces in the cooking. The liquid should cover all the solids by about an inch. It should not be pasty, but of the nature of broth gravy, and have a reddish hue from the chili pepper and tomatoes. The stew is improved by a bunch of parsley chopped fine and added just before serving, and a few sprigs of parsley may be used for garnishing. Serve hot with vegetables whole as far as possible. Any fresh meat and any vegetable may be used in this stew.

Spareribs (for 60 men).

    40 pounds spareribs.

Cut into pieces of about three ribs each. Wash clean and place in boiler, pour over them sufficient water to just cover; let them come to a boil, then drain off the water. Place in a bake pan about 3 inches deep; highly season with pepper, salt, and a little sage, stir and baste frequently. The oven should not be quite as hot as for beef. The ribs should be cooked well done. They may be parboiled, rolled in egg batter, and then fried in deep grease. They may also be served with sauerkraut; add the ribs about an hour before the kraut is done; thoroughly mix with the kraut to impart a better flavor.

Stew, chop suey (for 60 men).

    15 pounds meat, cut in strips one-fourth inch thick and
        1 inch long.

    10 pounds onions, sliced.

    4 stalks celery, sliced crosswise.

    ½ pint barbecue sauce.

    2 gallons beef stock.

Braise meat, then add stock; let simmer from one-half to two hours. Thirty minutes before serving add onions, celery, and seasoning. This should be served with 5 pounds of rice.

Barbecue sauce (for 60 men).

    1 pound onions, browned to a crisp.

    3 ounces salt.

    1 quart vinegar.

    1 ounce ginger, nutmeg, allspice, all combined.

    ¾ ounce red pepper.

    1 can tomatoes.

    1 ounce saltpeter.

Mix all the above ingredients. Burn enough sugar to blacken 1½ quarts of water; it must be very black. Pour the blackened water over the whole and let come to a boil. Set in a cold place and, after the mixture has cooled, add 2 ounces of sugar. It costs about 20 cents to make 1 gallon of this sauce.

Stew, beef, Irish (for 60 men).

    15 pounds beef.

    13 pounds potatoes, peeled.

    2 pounds onions.

    ½ pound flour.

Select cuts of beef suitable for stewing and boiling; dice into half inch cubes, or smaller, cutting all about the same size. Place in cold water and bring all to the boiling point slowly. Cook at a simmering temperature until well done. Dice the potatoes into 1-inch cubes, chop the onions and add both to the meat. It may be necessary to add beef stock or water, which should cover the ingredients in the pan about 1 inch. Season with salt and pepper and thicken with batter made of flour, stew slowly until the vegetables are thoroughly done. The stew will be improved by the addition of 2 pounds of diced carrots or turnips, or 2 cans of tomatoes. To make a pot pie out of this, add the dough for the covering soon after the vegetables come to a boil. Bake in a 15-count oven. To improve the appearance, the dough may be washed with a beaten egg, which will give it a golden brown color. With the above recipe, many kinds of fillings and condiments may be used. Serve hot in soup tureens.

Tamales (for 60 men).
 8 pounds meat scraps.
 1 pound corn meal.
 5 pounds flour.
 5 pounds mashed potatoes.
 2 ounces salt.

Run the meat through a chopper and season with salt, chili pepper, oregano, comina seed, and garlic; moisten with beef stock. Meanwhile, make a stiff dough, using the flour and potatoes. Take about one-third of the dough and roll out on the table about the thickness of pie crust, using the corn meal for dusting; trim it on the side toward you and lay on the edge a roll of the mixture a little larger than the little finger; roll the dough about the meat and, when it meets, moisten slightly with water to make it hold together. Then cut from the sheet of dough remaining and repeat the operation. Cut the roll in pieces about as long as sausages and fry in deep lard. Serve hot with chili sauce.

Turkish stew (for 60 men).
 18 pounds raw lean meat.
 5 pounds rice.

Dice the meat into 1-inch cubes, roll in flour, and fry brown in a little grease. Brown a few onions and add to the meat, cover the whole with beef stock and season with cayenne pepper, salt, parsley, and a little garlic. Cook slowly on top of the range, or in the oven, for about two hours. Boil the rice until the grains may be crushed between the fingers, but still retain their original form; drain off all the water; make a border of rice around the platter, leaving a crater into which the stew is poured. Serve hot.

Venison roast (for 60 men).
 25 pounds venison, ham preferred.

Cut into pieces weighing about 5 pounds each; lard well every 2 inches, the strips of fat being well seasoned with pepper and salt, and, if desired, a little garlic, and roast in the same manner as beef, except that it should always be well done. Serve hot with gravy poured over it.

Other parts may be roasted in the same manner, but will require less cooking, according to the size of the pieces. Parts not suitable for roasts may be utilized in steaks, hash, stews, fritters, etc.

SAUCES FOR MEATS.

Cranberry sauce (for 60 men).

    10 quarts cranberries,

    2½ pounds sugar.

Wash and boil the berries well; put in a clean boiler with about 1 inch of water; cover tightly and boil until the berries break to pieces and cover themselves with their juice; remove the lid and let simmer in order to dry them out. Sweeten with sugar, boil about five minutes, and pour into an earthen or wooden vessel and cool. Serve cold with chicken or turkey, or nearly any kind of meat or cake.

Rhubarb sauce.

    20 pounds rhubarb.

Wash the rhubarb well and dice in one-half inch cubes and place in a clean boiler with about 1 inch of water; cover tightly and let steam slowly for about one and one-half hours. Then remove the lid and allow the water to evaporate for about an hour. Season with sugar and serve with cake or meat, or use for filling pies.

Tomato sauce.

    6 cans tomatoes.

    1 pound onions, chopped.

    ½ ounce cinnamon.

    1 ounce cloves.

    3 chili pods.

    2 ounces salt.

    2 ounces sugar.

    ½ pound butter.

    ½ pound flour.

Boil slowly all the ingredients, except the flour and butter, in 2 quarts of water for one and one-half hours. Remove from the range and run through a fine colander or sieve. Replace on the range and put the butter in a frying pan. When it becomes hot, add the flour, stir until smooth, and add to the sauce. Excellent for fish, meats, or croquettes. About 1 gallon.

FISH.

Baked fish (for 60 men).

    30 pounds fish.

    2 pounds bacon or salt pork.

Fish weighing from 5 pounds upward are preferred. Dress and place in a bake pan with three or four slices of bacon over each fish, and about 1 inch of water in the pan; season well with pepper and salt; place in a hot oven and bake one hour, basting frequently and allowing the oven to cool gradually while baking.

If desired, the entrails may be withdrawn from beneath the gills without cutting the belly open, and the fish filled with stuffing made by the recipe given in the Chicken, roast recipe on page 144.

Codfish, salt, boiled (for 60 men).

    20 pounds salt codfish.

Break the fish into pieces weighing about 2 ounces each; allow to boil for 15 minutes to remove the salt, change the water and boil until done, ordinarily about 30 minutes. Serve hot with cream sauce.

Codfish cakes (for 60 men).

    10 pounds salt codfish.

    10 pounds potatoes, mashed.

    12 eggs.

If whole cod is used, soak, boil, remove the bones, and pass through a meat chopper; mix with the potatoes and eggs; season to taste with pepper and salt, and mold into cakes weighing about 3 ounces each. Roll in cracker crumbs or flour and fry in deep fat. Serve hot with tomato gravy. These cakes may be improved by dipping in egg batter before frying.

Cream sauce for codfish (for 60 men).

    1 pound fat, butter preferred.

    4 cans evaporated milk.

    ½ pound onions, minced,

    ½ pound pickles, minced.

    6 hard boiled eggs, minced if desired.

Thicken 1 gallon of boiling water with a flour batter and season well with pepper and salt; let come to a boil and add the fat, milk, onions, and pickles; whip well and spread over the fish on the platter. The sauce may be improved by the addition of 6 hard-boiled eggs, chopped fine.

Fried fresh fish (for 60 men).
   30 pounds fresh fish.
Clean and slice (or split) into pieces not more than 1 inch thick; season with salt and pepper, roll in flour and corn meal, and fry in deep lard until thoroughly browned. Serve hot with salad or pickles and, if practicable, tomato or Worcestershire sauce.

Oysters, fried (for 60 men).
   360 oysters (6 to 8 quarts, according to size).
   18 eggs.
   4 pounds cracker meal.
Remove from can, or shells, and dry with a cloth; dip in egg batter and drop in a pan with cracker dust. After enough have been dropped in, shake pan well; take each one between the hands, press flat, and lay in the frying pan. Fry until slightly brown. Serve hot with tomato or Worcestershire sauce, and, if practicable, with slaw or salad.

Oysters, scalloped (for 60 men).
   12 quarts oysters, or about six for each man.
   3 pounds bacon, or butter if desired.
   2 cans evaporated milk.
   6 pounds bread, diced and toasted.
Dice the bacon and fry until crisp; add the oysters, allow to come to a boil and add the bread. Let stand about 15 or 20 minutes at very near boiling point and add the cream just before serving.

Salmon cakes (for 60 men).
   12 cans salmon.
   25 pounds mashed potatoes.
Mix well, adding a little beef stock and flour; season with salt and pepper; make into cakes of about 3 ounces each, roll in flour, fry in hot fat, and serve hot with tomato gravy or tomato sauce.

Salmon hash (for 60 men).

>   12 cans salmon.
>   25 pounds mashed potatoes.

Mix well, adding a little beef stock; spread 3 inches deep or less in a bake pan (slightly greased); season with salt and pepper, and allow to bake in a medium oven for 40 minutes or an hour. Serve hot.

Spanish fish sauce (for 60 men).

>   1 pound fat.
>   2 pounds minced onions.
>   4 minced tomatoes.
>   4 cloves garlic.
>   4 ounces chili colorado.
>   2 gallons beef stock.

Mix the onions, tomatoes, garlic, and chili; fry in grease until well done; add 2 gallons of beef stock and boil about 10 minutes, thicken slightly with a flour batter, and season with salt to taste. Serve hot over the fish. This sauce may also be used for boiled or baked fish and various kinds of meats.

VEGETABLES.

Beans, baked (for 60 men).

>   15 pounds beans, issue.
>   2 pounds bacon, diced.
>   5 ounces sugar, or
>   ½ pint molasses.

Wash the beans thoroughly in cold water; drain and place in cold water and boil 15 minutes; drain again and place the bacon, beans, sugar (or molasses), 5 gallons of water, and salt to taste in the boiler or jar; place on the range and let come to a boil; after about 15 minutes, cover with a lid and place in the oven. If the beans are to be served for dinner, the above work should be attended to the preceding evening, and the fire should be left so as to keep up a slow heat for the greater part of the night. The first thing in the morning more water should be put in (if necessary), covering the beans about 1 inch. It the breakfast requires a hot fire, the oven door should be left partly open, so that the beans will only simmer. If the oven can not be thus regulated, the beans should be removed and placed on the range or mantel, where they will barely simmer. It may be necessary to add more water several times in the course of the morning (in order to keep the beans barely covered). By 10 o'clock in the morning there should be sufficient juice in the kettle, so that bubbles will rise to the surface as the beans simmer; in one-half hour the beans will be ready to serve and should be removed to a place where they will be kept warm. Serve hot with some kind of salad.

Water added while cooking should be boiling hot. Especially in summer, the beans should not be soaked, as they may sour and have a bad flavor. Beans left over may be used in the preparation of bean salad or chili con carne.

Beans, lima (for 60 men).
   12 pounds lima beans.
   ½ pound of flour.
   1 pound bacon, diced.

Wash the beans thoroughly; place in a boiler with about 5 gallons of water; boil 10 minutes and pour off the water; add the flour and bacon and mix well; salt and pepper to taste; add about 4 gallons of water, and allow to simmer until well done. Serve hot.

The flour is used for the purpose of keeping the beans whole while cooking. Time required to prepare, about four hours.

Beans cooked in a trench. This is an excellent method when properly done. Prepare the beans in the same manner as if they were to be baked in the Army range in garrison. Dig a trench about 6 inches deeper and 6 inches wider than the camp kettles used, and long enough to allow 6 inches between kettles and between kettles and ends of trench. Build a good fire in the trench and let it bum to coals. Take out two-thirds of the coals, permitting one-third to remain in the trench. Place the camp kettles with lids on in the trench, resting on the coals. Fill in the space between kettles and at the ends of the trench with coal and earth, placing hot coals next to the kettles. Fill in well and cover the kettles to a depth of about 8 inches, about 3 inches of coal and 5 inches of earth, the latter being on top. If this is done about 7 o'clock in the evening, the beans should be cooked by 4 o'clock in the morning. The same cook who has placed the kettles in the trench and covered them should dig them out in the morning, as he will understand better how the lids are set and there will be less danger of getting dirt in the kettles. Sufficient beans should be cooked for breakfast and lunch. If on the march, the beans for lunch should be issued to the men to be carried in their individual mess kits.

Beets, boiled (for 60 men).

22 pounds beets.

Wash the beets thoroughly and boil until well done; hold under a faucet and rub the skins off with the hands; cut into slices, or if young and tender, they may be served whole. Serve hot with cream sauce or gravy poured over them. While washing and cooking be careful not to break the skins.

Cabbage, Bavarian (for 60 men).

30 pounds cabbage.

5 pounds salt pork, or sliced bacon.

1 quart vinegar.

Strip off the outer leaves and cut out the cores; cut up as for sauerkraut; wash and place in a boiler; add the salt pork (or bacon), vinegar, and a gallon of water; season with salt and pepper; boil slowly in an open boiler for three hours, adding boiling water if necessary; then thicken slightly with a flour batter and boil about five minutes longer, when it will be ready to serve.

Cabbage, fried (for 60 men).

22 pounds cooked cabbage.

2 pounds bacon drippings.

Chop the cabbage fine and add the bacon drippings; season with salt and pepper; set on a range in a covered pan and fry about one-half hour, stirring frequently to prevent burning.

Carrots, mashed (for 60 men).

22 pounds carrots.

4 quarts beef stock.

1 pound bacon drippings.

Peel the carrots and cut into slices not more than one-half inch thick; place in an open boiler and pour in the beef stock; season with salt and pepper; cook slowly until thoroughly done. Add the bacon drippings and mash thoroughly. Serve hot.

Carrots may also be used in various other dishes, such as beef à la mode, beef soup, vegetable soup, etc.

Corn, canned (for 60 men).

> 10 No. 2 cans corn.
> 4 quarts beef stock.
> 2 ounces sugar.
> 1 1-pound can evaporated milk.

Remove from the cans and place in a boiler; add the beef stock (strained), sugar, and milk; season to taste with salt, and mix well. Place on the range where not too hot and allow to come almost to a boil; thicken slightly with a flour batter, and allow to remain on the range for 15 minutes until it comes almost to a boil, when it will be ready to serve.

Corn, green (for 60 men).

> 180 ears.

Remove the husks and trim the ends; brush the silk off with a new scrubbing brush; place in well-salted boiling water and boil about 20 minutes. Serve with butter, if practicable.

Egg plant (for 60 men).

> 20 pounds egg plant.
> 5 eggs.

Peel the egg plant and slice lengthwise; beat the eggs well and add to them about 1½ pints of water; season the egg plant with salt and dip in the egg and water mixture; roll in flour and place on a board lightly covered with flour; remove with a cake turner and try in deep grease until browned; place on a platter and drain off the fat well before serving.

Greens (for 60 men).

> 30 pounds greens.
> 5 pounds bacon.

Put the greens and bacon in 2 gallons of water, and boil in an open boiler for about two hours; remove the bacon and strain the water from the greens; chop fine and place in a well-greased bake pan; add beef stock to moisten and bake in the oven for about one-half hour; salt and pepper to taste; slice the bacon and serve on top of the greens. Greens may be improved by the addition of minced hard-boiled eggs.

Asparagus, beets, cabbage, dandelion, spinach, and other greens may be prepared according to the above recipe, but the time required for cooking will depend upon the particular kind of greens used. Cabbage greens in particular require more cooking than others.

Hominy (for 60 men).
> 6 pounds fine hominy.
> 1 ounce salt.

Place 4 gallons of water in a boiler on the range; when boiling, add the hominy and salt; boil from 20 to 30 minutes; remove to the end of the range and let simmer for half an hour. Serve with milk.

Macaroni and cheese (for 60 men).
> 6 pounds macaroni.
> 2 pounds cheese, diced.

Add the macaroni to 4 gallons of boiling water, salted to taste; boil about 20 minutes, but not until it becomes flabby; strain the water off; spread about one-third of the macaroni in the bottom of a well-greased bake pan; then, one-third of the diced cheese on the macaroni; continue the alternate layers until all are in the bake pan. Bake in the oven about 30 minutes and serve hot.

If desired, 2 or 3 pounds of toasted bread crumbs and 2 or 3 cans of tomatoes may be mixed with the cheese between the layers of macaroni.

Onions, boiled (for 60 men).
> 22 pounds onions.

Select onions not more than half as large as eggs; boil from one-half to three-fourths of an hour and serve with cream sauce. Left-over boiled onions may be used in making gravy, hash, stewed potatoes, or Lyonnaise potatoes.

Onions, stuffed (for 60 men).
> 15 pounds onions, medium size.
> 3 pounds toasted bread crumbs.
> 8 pounds meat scraps.
> 8 pounds bread scraps.

Peel the onions with a sharp knife and dig out the center from the top end, leaving a shell. Meanwhile prepare a dressing, using the meat and bread, and stuff each onion full. Sprinkle the toasted bread crumbs in a well-greased bake pan and place the onions in the pan; grease well over the top and bake 40 minutes in a medium oven. Serve hot with chili or tomato sauce poured over it.

The above preparation may be used as the meat component of a meal if desired.

Parsnips, baked (for 60 men).
    22 pounds parsnips.
    1 quart beef stock.
    3 pounds bacon.
Scrape and wash the parsnips thoroughly and place in a well-greased bake pan; season with pepper and salt and pour the beef stock over them; place strips of bacon over the parsnips and cover with a pan to prevent evaporation; place in the oven and bake slowly until thoroughly done.

Parsnips may also be used in beef and vegetable soups. This is not recommended, as they give a strong flavor.

Peas, canned (for 60 men).
    10 No. 2 cans peas.
    ½ pound butter.
Empty the peas into a stew pot; pepper and salt to taste and add the butter; allow to come to a boil, thicken slightly with a flour batter, and let come to a boil again, when they will be ready to serve.

Peas, green (for 60 men).
    10 quarts green peas.
    5 quarts beef stock.
    1 pound butter or drippings.
    3 cans evaporated milk.
Carefully pick over and place in a boiler or stew pot; add the beef stock and butter; season with salt and pepper and boil about 15 minutes; thicken with a flour batter and let come to a boil again. Add milk if available, and the peas are ready to serve.

Potatoes, browned (for 60 men).
    22 pounds potatoes.
Select the small potatoes; wash and boil until done; peel and then grease each potato; spread over the bottom of a well-greased bake pan in a single layer; and bake in a brisk oven until brown, usually about 30 minutes.

Potato cakes (for 60 men).

    22 pounds potatoes.

    1 pound flour.

    2 ounces green chopped parsley.

Run the potatoes through a meat chopper, and roll into cakes weighing about 3 ounces each; roll in flour and fry in deep lard until nicely browned; serve as a vegetable with any kind of meat. Leftover potatoes prepared in any manner may be used in this recipe.

Potatoes, cheesed (for 60 men).

    22 pounds potatoes.

    1 gallon beef stock.

    1 pound grated cheese.

Use any left-over cooked potatoes; cut about the size of a lima bean; season with salt and pepper; mix with the beef stock; add the grated cheese. Spread 2 or 3 inches deep over the bottom of a well-greased bake pan and bake for about 30 minutes in a quick oven.

Potatoes, creamed (for 60 men).

    22 pounds potatoes.

    1 gallon beef stock.

    1 can evaporated milk.

    2 ounces parsley.

Boil the potatoes until well done; peel and slice crosswise; allow the beef stock to come to a boil on the range; thicken with a flour batter and add the evaporated milk; place the potatoes in a bake pan and pour the mixture over them, it being just sufficient in quantity to cover the potatoes. Allow to come to a boil and remove from the range immediately. Meanwhile, chop the parsley very fine and, before serving, sprinkle evenly over the potatoes. Salt to taste.

Potatoes, French fried (for 60 men).

    22 pounds potatoes, peeled.

Cut lengthwise into one-half inch slices, and fry in deep lard until nicely browned; after frying, dust slightly with salt, and serve hot with any kind of meat.

On account of the quantity of potatoes to be prepared for an organization mess, it is not advisable to cut in thin slices, as is usually done. This is a dish much relished by the men, and on account of its comparative cheapness it is recommended for frequent use.

In many kitchens they are considered too expensive, because it is believed that a large amount of lard or other fat is required to fry them. Experiments have proven conclusively that, while considerable lard or fat is required to float them, a very small amount is actually consumed in frying. In recent experiments with pure lard, it was found that only 10 ounces were used in frying 17 pounds of potatoes. One pound of refined cottonseed oil will fry 25 pounds of potatoes.

Potatoes, French baked (for 60 men).
> 22 pounds of potatoes.
> 1 pound fat.
> 2 quarts stock.

Wash, peel, and slice potatoes as for French fried. Place in a well-greased bake pan. Salt to taste. Add stock and fat. Mix thoroughly. Place in medium oven and bake about one hour, or until done. During the process of cooking they should not be disturbed with forks or spoons, but should be, when served, as nearly as possible in the same form as when first placed in the pan. Serve hot.

Potatoes, German boiled (for 60 men).
> 22 pounds potatoes.
> 1 pound onions, browned.

Cut the potatoes into pieces about the size of an egg; place in cool water and boil slowly until done; place in vegetable dishes and over each place about two basting spoonfuls of browned onion. Serve hot. Potatoes left over from this recipe may be used in Lyonnaise potatoes, salads, fried potatoes, hash, stews, and various other ways.

Potatoes, hashed (for 60 men).
> 22 pounds potatoes.
> 1 gallon beef stock.

Cut the cooked potatoes into pieces about the size of a lima bean; season with salt and pepper, and mix with beef stock the same as when making hash; spread 2 or 3 inches deep over the bottom of a well-greased bake pan; spread a little fat over the top and bake for about 30 minutes in a quick oven.

Potatoes, Lyonnaise (for 60 men).
    22 pounds potatoes.
    2 pounds onions.
Wash the potatoes and boil them until they may be easily pierced with a fork; peel and slice crosswise; wash and slice the onions, fry brown and add the potatoes. Season with pepper and salt, adding sufficient fat to moisten, and spread about 2 inches deep in the bottom of a well-greased bake pan. Bake about 30 minutes in a quick oven.

Potatoes, sweet, baked (for 60 men).
    22 pounds sweet potatoes.
Wash well and remove all defective spots; place in a bake pan and cover with a second pan to prevent evaporation while baking, and bake until well done, usually about 35 minutes.

If desired, the potatoes may be peeled, rolled in fat, and lightly sprinkled with sugar and salt before baking.

Potatoes, sweet, candied (for 60 men).
    20 pounds sweet potatoes.
    1 pound butter
    1 pound sugar.
    1 gallon beef stock, strained.
Wash the potatoes and boil until fairly well done; peel and slice lengthwise, spread in three layers in a bake pan, putting about one-third of the sugar and butter on top of each layer; pour the beef stock over the whole and bake in a medium hot oven for 40 minutes or an hour.

Pumpkin, baked (for 60 men).
    22 pounds pumpkin.
    1 pound bacon drippings.
Peel the pumpkin, remove the seeds and clean well; cut in pieces not more than 2 inches square; spread these, in one layer, in a bake pan and pour over them about one pound of bacon drippings; season with salt and pepper; cover with a larger pan to prevent evaporation and bake in a slow oven until well done. Or select pumpkins about 5 pounds each; split in halves and clean well, without peeling; sprinkle with salt and sugar and place in a bake pan, with the cut side up. Bake in a slow oven until thoroughly done.

Rice, fried (for 60 men).

> 5 pounds rice.
>
> 2 pounds fat.
>
> 1 pound onions, diced.

When the water comes to a boil, add the rice and salt. When the rice may be mashed in the fingers, pour into a colander and drain well, after which each grain should be whole and separate. Place the fat in a bake pan; set on the range and let come to a smoking temperature; add the onions and let them brown slightly; add the rice and stir continually with a cake turner to prevent burning and to mix the grease with it thoroughly. Rice may be cooked in a hot oven, but must be stirred every few minutes. About 15 or 20 minutes are required to fry it. It may be served with beef curry, Turkish stew, or as a vegetable.

Sauerkraut (for 60 men).

> 5 gallons sauerkraut.
>
> 3 gallons beef stock.

Season to taste and allow to simmer for about two hours. Sauerkraut should be cooked with some kind of meat.

How to make sauerkraut (one gallon).

> 7¼ pounds trimmed cabbage.
>
> 4 ounces salt.

Remove outer green leaves, and after slicing the cabbage fine with cutter, place in barrel and salt; then, with a large wooden masher, stamp until of a mushy consistency. More cabbage and salt may be added and the operation continued until the barrel is full. After the barrel is filled cover the kraut with a clean cloth and then with a board prepared to fit snugly inside of the barrel. The board will be placed on the cloth and a hundred-pound rock on the board while the cabbage is fermenting. Let stand in a temperature of about 70° F. for one month. If the kraut is made in warm weather, the amount of salt used must be increased to 6 ounces per gallon, and the time it takes for it to ripen will be less than in colder weather. When the kraut is ready for use it will have a decided odor, but when not fully matured it will have an odor somewhat resembling that of beer. The temperature of the place where it is stored has much to do in influencing the acidity acquired in any given time. Each time when removing kraut from barrel, thoroughly wash both cloth and barrel cover, as well as weight and sides of barrel, before replacing. This should be attended to once each week whether kraut is removed or not. Care should be exercised in the selection of a barrel for sauerkraut. Charred barrels should not he used. Oak barrels are preferable.

Squash, mashed (for 60 men).

    15 pounds squash.

    2 quarts beef stock.

    1 pound bacon drippings.

Peel the squash, remove the seeds and clean well; cut in pieces not more than 2 inches square; place in a boiler and pour over it the beef stock; season with salt and pepper; close the boiler with a tight lid and boil for about two hours (or until well done); add the bacon drippings, and mash well before serving.

Succotash (for 60 men).

    1½ gallons corn, cut from the cob.

    1½ gallons cooked lima beans.

    1 pound bacon, diced.

Mix the corn, beans, and bacon; season to taste; pour over the mixture sufficient beef stock to cover it; place in the oven and stew for 30 minutes; thicken slightly with a flour batter and boil for 5 minutes more, when it will be ready to serve.

Tomatoes, stewed (for 60 men).

    20 pounds tomatoes.

Place 8 or 10 tomatoes in a colander at a time, and set in boiling water for about one-half minute; peel, split in halves, and place in the stewpot, stew for one-half hour and add 2 quarts of strained beef stock; season with pepper and salt; and add bread crumbs, if desired.

Stewed canned tomatoes.—Take six small cans tomatoes; remove from the cans, place in the stewpot and add 2 ounces of sugar and one-half pound of bacon drippings; pepper and salt to taste, and, if desired, add bread and beef stock, place on the range, allow to come to a boil and serve immediately.

SALADS AND DRESSINGS.

Salads are easily prepared and, when well seasoned and served, meet with much favor. In addition to the ingredients, a little forethought is necessary as the different components should be prepared some time in advance.

Certain fundamental principles must be observed in their preparation:

1. Salads must be served cold.

2. They should be highly seasoned.

3. They should be attractively served. To accomplish this almost any bits of sightly tender vegetables may be placed about the dish or on top or the salad. Sprigs of parsley, lettuce, either whole or shredded, celery, green onions, sliced unpeeled radishes, diamond or heart shaped beets, sliced pickles or lemons, shredded cabbage, minced pickles shaken over the salad, are all used.

Any vegetable may be used in salads, either alone or in combination with other vegetables. Lettuce, radishes, and onions may be used in several combinations. Cabbage, shredded fine and soaked in cold water for two hours, makes a satisfactory salad. Stringless beans or peas that have been cooked and cooled may be used alone or in combination with other vegetables. An excellent salad may be made of beets, either alone or preferably combined with other vegetables. The beets should be cooked, then diced and allowed to stand in vinegar for one hour. Potatoes are frequently used in salads, either alone or as a filler in meat, fish, or vegetable salads.

When meat salads are served to troops a vegetable filler should be added to diminish the cost and improve the flavor. Thus, when chicken is provided, one-half boneless chicken and one-half diced celery or other green vegetables should be used. Turkey, tongue, lean beef cut fine may be used. All meat must be well done before using. Fat meat is undesirable as the dressing usually contains olive or cottonseed oil in such quantity that other fats are unnecessary.

Almost any kind of edible fish may be used in salad, although large fish are to be preferred on account of being more easily boned. Fish should be cooked until done, the bones removed, and the flesh mixed with one-third to one-half vegetables. Cold hard-boiled eggs, olives, onions, or pickles, minced or sliced when mixed in a salad, spread over it, or used as a garnish, add to the appearance and flavor.

Apple and celery salad (for 60 men).
>   6 pounds apples.
>   6 pounds celery.
>   3 pints mayonnaise dressing.

Keep the celery in a damp cloth so that it will be crisp. When ready for use cut it into one-half inch pieces. Peel and core the apples, and just before adding them to the mixture, cut them into pieces similar in size to the celery. Add half the mayonnaise dressing and mix well.

Serve on garnished vegetable dishes, with half the dressing spread on the top.

Bean salad (for 60 men).

    15 pounds baked beans.

    3 pounds onions, chopped fine.

    2 pounds pickles, chopped fine.

Mix thoroughly and season with salt, pepper, mustard, and vinegar. Baked beans left over from dinner are frequently available for salads.

Celery salad (for 60 men).

    12 pounds celery, diced fine.

    2 pounds mashed potatoes.

    2 pounds bacon grease or olive oil.

    1 pint vinegar.

    1 pint water.

    2 ounces mustard.

    12 hard-boiled eggs (if desired).

Dice the celery fine, chop the eggs, and mix the two together. For the dressing, mash the potatoes thoroughly, add the bacon grease (or olive oil) with the vinegar very slowly, and add a little salt, with cayenne pepper and mustard. The sauce should then be of the consistency of cream or gravy.

Chicken salad (for 60 men).

    30 pounds chicken.

    2 bunches celery, diced.

    1½ pints olive oil.

    1 quart vinegar.

    2 ounces mustard.

    1 pound mashed potatoes.

Wash the chicken thoroughly, place in boiling water, and boil until the meat may be easily separated from the bones. Run the meat through the chopper, and when cold, add the diced celery. Mix the mustard, olive oil, potatoes, and vinegar and pour over the salad; mix well and season with pepper and salt. May be served with or without mayonnaise dressing.

Crab salad (for 60 men).
  6 cans salted crabs.
  12 pounds celery, diced.
  ½ pound onions, chopped.
  ½ pint olive oil, or
  ½ pound bacon, diced and browned.
  1 pint vinegar.
  1 ounce mustard.
  ½ pound mashed potatoes.

Place the crabs, onions, and celery in a chopping bowl or dish pan; add the mustard, olive oil, and vinegar to the potatoes, and whip well; pour the mixture over the salad and mix well. Cabbage may be substituted for the celery, and bacon for the olive oil.

French dressing (for 60 men).
  3 teaspoonsful salt.
  ¼ teaspoonful pepper, cayenne.
  1 pint cottonseed oil.
  1 pint vinegar.

Put the salt, pepper, and oil in a dish and beat thoroughly. When thick and creamy, add slowly the vinegar. This dressing should lot be poured over the salad until immediately before it is to be eaten.

Lettuce salad (for 60 men).
  20 pounds lettuce.
  6 hard-boiled eggs, minced fine.
  1 pound bacon, diced and browned.
  1 quart vinegar.

Wash and clean lettuce thoroughly; mix the bacon, mustard, minced eggs, vinegar, and a little pepper and salt, and pour over the lettuce when cold. Serve ice cold.

Lobster salad (for 60 men).

> 12 cans lobsters.
> 12 pounds celery, diced,
> ½ pound bacon or olive oil.
> ½ pound onions, chopped.
> 1 pint vinegar.
> 1 ounce mustard,
> ½ pound mashed potatoes.

Mix the lobsters, onions, and celery in a chopping bowl or dishpan; add the mustard, olive oil, and vinegar to the potatoes and whip well; pour the mixture over the salad and mix well.

Cabbage may be substituted for the celery, and bacon for the olive oil, if desired. If bacon is used, it should be fried to a crisp before mixing with other ingredients.

Piccalilli salad (for 60 men).

> 3 pounds cabbage, minced.
> 3 quarts tomatoes, minced.
> 3 pounds onions, minced.
> 3 pounds pickles, issue, minced.
> ½ quart vinegar.

Mix all the ingredients well; season with salt, cayenne pepper, and cloves, and add sufficient water to make 2 gallons. Serve with baked beans or meat of any kind.

Pimento salad (for 60 men).

> 6 one-pound cans pimentos.
> 8 pounds cabbage.
> 1 pound pickles, issue.
> 1 quart mayonnaise dressing.

Shred cabbage fine and place in cold salt water for an hour. Select one-fourth of the pimentos best for the purpose and slice them into fine cords like shoe strings. Chop remaining pimentos fine; shake water from cabbage and place in salad bowls with the chopped pimentos, the pickles, and one-third the mayonnaise, and mix well, place the mixture in cold vegetable dishes. Spread the remainder of the mayonnaise and pimento on top and serve immediately.

Potato salad (for 60 men).

>   20 pounds potatoes, boiled and sliced.
>   1 pound onions, minced.
>   1 pound bacon, diced and browned,
>   1 pint water.
>   1 pint vinegar.

Place the potatoes in a chopping bowl with the onions over them. Fry the bacon until brown, and while still hot dash over the potatoes, and add the vinegar and water. Mix well, pepper and salt to taste, and allow to stand for two hours before serving.

Salmon salad (for 60 men).

>   6 one-pound cans salmon.
>   4 pounds boiled potatoes, diced.
>   4 pounds lettuce.
>   1 quart mayonnaise dressing.

Cool the cans and empty contents into a salad bowl, chop fine, and mix with the potatoes. Soak the lettuce in cold salt water for one hour, remove and shake well. Shred with a sharp knife and add to the salad. Mix one-third of the mayonnaise with the salad and spread the remainder over the surface. Garnish with sprigs of tender vegetables and serve immediately.

Slaw (for 60 men).

>   30 pounds cabbage.
>   2 pounds bacon, diced and browned,
>   1½ quarts vinegar.
>   6 pounds onions.

Wash the cabbage thoroughly and chop fine; add the onions, bacon, and vinegar, and season with pepper and salt. Mix thoroughly and let come to a boil in a closed vessel, when it will be ready to serve. Serve hot or cold.

Sour cream dressing for slaw (for 60 men).

    1 pint vinegar.

    1 pint milk.

    ¼ pint oil or four ounces of butter, melted.

    2 teaspoonsful mustard.

    4 teaspoonsful salt.

    ⅛ teaspoonful cayenne pepper.

    4 teaspoonsful sugar.

Add the vinegar to the milk, then the oil, then the other ingredients, stirring with a wire beater. Add to the slaw just before serving.

DESSERTS.

Apple rolls (for 60 men).

    6 pounds flour.

    3 pounds lard.

    1½ gallons stewed apples.

Prepare the dough as for pies, and the apples as for apple pies, but a little drier; roll the dough out into strips about 7 inches wide and a little longer than the width of the pan; raise the farther end of the pan about 4 inches from the table; spread one of the strips of dough across the lower end of the pan and place the apples for one roll on this strip; fold the farther side of the strip of dough over toward you and then fold the nearer side from you, tucking it under the roll. Continue making the rolls in the same manner, rolling them up like a cigarette, and placing each in succession beyond the one previously made. When the pan is filled, trim off the ends with a knife. In no case should the rolls be over 3 inches thick. Bake about 40 minutes in a 15-count oven and cut lengthwise of the pan into pieces about 3 inches long. Serve hot or cold with a cream sauce, in vegetable dishes.

Any kind of stewed fruit may be substituted for the apples and the rolls named accordingly.

Apple cobbler (for 60 men).

    4 pounds evaporated apples.

    6 pounds sugar.

    1 ounce cinnamon.

    1 grated nutmeg.

Wash the apples thoroughly and soak them in cold water for two hours, then cook in 1½ gallons of water until well done, but not broken. Let cool; then add sugar and spices.

Crust to be made as follows:

8 pounds flour.

4 ounces baking powder.

1 pound lard.

1 pound sugar.

16 eggs.

1½ ounces salt.

1 quart and 1 gill of water.

Cream the sugar, lard, and salt thoroughly; then add the eggs, one at a time, stirring constantly. Pour in the water and mix well. Sift the flour and baking powder together several times; then add them to the mixture and work until smooth.

Take about two-thirds of the dough and roll out one-half inch thick. Line two bake pans and bake in a 15-count oven for 20 minutes. When baked cover both crusts in pans with cold fruit about one-half inch thick. Roll out the remainder of the dough and, with it, cover the contents of both pans, tucking the sides down well. Bake for 20 minutes on the oven shelf in an 18-count oven.

Serve cold with the following sauce:

1 gallon water.

1½ pounds sugar.

3 ounces cornstarch.

1 nutmeg, grated.

Any fruit may be used. Fresh fruit is preferable.

Brown Betty (for 60 men).

9 pounds bread or bread scraps.

6 pounds caramelized sugar.

2 pounds currants or other dried tart fruit.

Dice the bread into 1-inch cubes and brown in a slow oven; place 3 gallons of water on the range and add the caramelized sugar and the fruit; thicken slightly with a flour batter; pour over the diced toast. Let cook in the oven about 20 minutes and serve with plain sauce.

Cake, corn (for 60 men).

    5 pounds flour.

    3 pounds corn meal.

    4 pounds sugar.

    2 pounds fat.

    16 eggs.

    7 ounces baking powder.

    ½ ounce extract.

    1½ ounces salt.

Whip the sugar, fat, extract, and salt to a cream, and add the eggs slowly; then add the flour, corn meal, baking powder, and sufficient water to make a stiff batter. Bake in an 18-count oven for about 40 minutes. This cake may be made in different forms, using the biscuit molds as well as bake pans.

Fruit cake, dark.

    2½ pounds sugar.

    2½ pounds butter, fresh.

    25 eggs, whole.

    7 ounces molasses, sorghum.

    3¾ pounds flour.

    ¼ ounce nutmeg.

    ¼ ounce cinnamon.

    ¼ ounce ginger.

    ¼ ounce cloves,

    1½ pounds citron.

    5 ounces lemon peel.

    5 ounces orange peel.

    2½ pounds raisins.

    2½ pounds currants,

    1½ pounds mixed nuts, shelled.

    ½ pint brandy or cream.

Slice citron, lemon, and orange peel very thin and about the size of a postage stamp. Then wash in luke-warm water and rinse in clean, luke-warm water. Pick the raisins and currants and nuts over carefully and then wash and rinse them in the same way. When all the fruit is cleanly washed, mix and put in a sieve to drain for about 2 hours. Then mix in the nutmeg, ginger, cloves, cinnamon, and 12 ounces of flour. The flour is put in to keep the fruit separated and to keep it from settling to the bottom.

Cream the sugar and butter well, then add the eggs, one at a time, stirring constantly. Next add the molasses, stirring it in, then the brandy or cream and, after this, the 3 pounds of flour. When the flour is about half mixed in the batter, add the dredged fruit and spices and continue mixing until the fruit is evenly distributed and the mixture smooth. This mixture makes 21 pounds of cake.

The best results are obtained by baking fruit cake in an earthen crock. If this is not available it may be baked in a pan. Fruit cake requires a long, slow process of baking. An average of 1 hour per pound in a 20-count oven is required for small cakes.

Cake, layer (for 60 men).

> 2 pounds lard, butter, or drippings.
> 4 pounds sugar.
> 16 eggs.
> ½ ounce extract.
> 8 pounds flour.
> 6 ounces baking powder.

Beat the lard, sugar, eggs, and extract together for about 10 minutes, and add the flour, baking powder, and sufficient milk or water to make a stiff batter. Bake about 20 minutes in a 15-count oven. The name given the cake will depend upon the kind of filling used between the layers.

Cake, plain (for 60 men).

> 6 pounds flour.
> 3 pounds sugar.
> 2 pounds butter, lard, or drippings.
> 5 ounces baking powder.
> 8 eggs.
> 1 ounce salt,
> ½ ounce extract.

Break the eggs in a wooden bowl with the lard, sugar, extract, and salt, and whip to a cream; sift the flour in on top of the mixture and the baking powder on top of the flour, mixing the baking powder slightly with the flour without disturbing the mixture below. Add sufficient water to make a stiff batter; place in well-greased bake pans with greased papers over the bottom; bake about 40 minutes in an 18-count oven. Do not remove from the pans until cold (about 2 hours); otherwise it will break. This cake may be served with a sauce as cottage pudding.

Raised cake.
> 1 pound raised dough.
> 12 ounces lard or butter,
> 24 ounces sugar.
> 6 eggs.
> ½ ounce soda, dissolved in 2 tablespoonsful of hot water.
> 1 pound flour.
> 1 ounce each nutmeg and cinnamon.
> ¼ ounce cloves.
> 1 pound raisins.

Take 1 pound of dough when it is ready to punch down the first time. Add to it the butter and sugar and mix well. Add the eggs, one at a time, working them into the dough; then the soda dissolved in hot water; then the flour. Sift the cinnamon, cloves, and nutmeg together and add to the mixture. After thoroughly working put in a bake pan or a 1-gallon crock. Place in a proof box for 1 hour. Bake in a 20-count oven for 2 hours. Let cool before removing from the pan.

Crullers, 1-pound mixture.
> 2 ounces butter.
> 4 ounces sugar.
> 2 eggs.
> ¹⁄₁₆ ounce extract.
> 1 pound flour.
> ½ ounce baking powder.
> ¼ pint water (good measure).

Cream butter and sugar together and add the extract. Beat the eggs well and add them to the mixture. Thoroughly mix the baking powder with the flour and sift on top of mixture; then add the water and stir until smooth. Roll out the dough to a thickness of half an inch and cut with doughnut cutter. Fry to a golden brown in deep grease. Immediately upon their removal from the fat, place the crullers in a colander to drain, after which they may be rolled in granulated sugar or placed on a plate and dusted with powdered sugar.

The same rule applies to this as to other baking powder mixtures; to obtain good results handle as little as possible. The quantity of the liquid used depends upon the strength of the flour. Baking powder may be increased or decreased in this mixture according to its strength as determined by experience.

If the dough is rolled to one-half inch thickness and cut with a 3½-inch cutter, the above mixture will make 19 crullers.

Custard (1 gallon).

> 1 quart eggs.
> 2 quarts milk.
> 2 pounds sugar.
> ¼ ounce extract.

Beat the eggs to a foam with the milk and sugar; pour in a well-greased bake pan and cook in a slow oven. If the eggs are not strictly fresh, it may be necessary to add about 2 ounces of corn starch to each gallon, and this is advisable in any case. The number of eggs may be reduced and the amount of corn starch correspondingly increased. Any flavoring may be used. Serve cold.

Fritters, corn (for 60 men).

> 2¼ pounds corn meal.
> 2 pounds sugar.
> 5 pounds flour.
> 4 ounces baking powder.
> 12 eggs.

Make into a soft dough; drop portions of uniform size from spoon into about 3 inches of smoking fat. Keep each fritter as nearly round as possible and have not more than two-thirds of the surface of the fat covered with fritters at a time.

Ice, lemon (1 gallon, for 20 men).

> 18 lemons.
> 1½ pounds sugar.
> 1 ounce gelatin.
> 3 quarts water.
> 1 teaspoonful lemon extract.

Squeeze the juice from the lemons and grate the rinds; add these and the gelatin and sugar to the water. Let come to a boil, cool, and add the extract and freeze.

Ice, orange (1 gallon, for 20 men).

>   12 oranges.
>
>   3 quarts water.
>
>   3 lemons.
>
>   1½ pounds sugar.
>
>   ¼ ounce orange extract.
>
>   1 ounce gelatin.

Squeeze the juice of the oranges and lemons into the water, at the same time adding the gelatin, three orange rinds, sugar, and the flavoring extract. Add sufficient water to make 1 gallon and freeze.

Ice, pineapple (1 gallon, for 20 men).

>   3 or 4 pineapples, according to size, or
>
>   2 No. 2 cans pineapples,
>
>   1½ pounds sugar.
>
>   2 quarts water.
>
>   1 ounce gelatin.

Place the water on the range and let it come to a boil; add the juice of the pineapple (if canned pineapples are used), and dice the pineapples to about the size of a bean, adding them together with the sugar and gelatin to the water. Allow to come to a boil, then cool and freeze.

Raspberries, gooseberries, strawberries, or any tart fruit may be used in the same way. If the fruit contains much acid, the amount of water used should be correspondingly increased.

Ice cream (1 gallon for 20 men).

>   3 ounces flour.
>
>   1½ pounds sugar.
>
>   10 eggs.
>
>   ¼ ounce extract.
>
>   2 cans evaporated milk.

Boil 2 quarts of water and add a batter made of the flour and 1 pint of water; then allow to come to a boil again; remove from the range, and add the sugar, eggs, a pinch of salt, flavoring extract, evaporated milk, and sufficient water to make 1 gallon. Whip well, and allow to cool before putting in the freezer.

Ice cream, chocolate (for 20 men).

    3 ounces chocolate grated.

    3 ounces flour.

    1½ pounds sugar.

    2 cans evaporated milk.

    10 eggs.

Put the grated chocolate in 2 quarts of water on the range and let come to a boil; add a batter made of the flour and a pint of water; let come to a boil again and remove from the range. Add the eggs and sugar; whip well and add the milk, together with sufficient water to make 1 gallon; allow to cool before putting in the freezer.

Ice cream, coffee (1 gallon, for 20 men).

    6 ounces coffee.

    1½ pounds sugar.

    4 to 10 eggs.

    2 cans evaporated milk.

    3 ounces flour.

Add the coffee to 1 quart of boiling water; then remove from the range, cover well, and allow to stand until cool. Make a batter of the flour and add 1 pint of water and place in a quart of water boiling on the range. Let come to a boil; remove from the range, and strain the coffee into the mixture through a clean cloth. Add the eggs, sugar, and cream. Whip well and add sufficient water to make 1 gallon. Freeze as ordinary ice cream.

Pie, apple.

    1 gallon stewed apples or 3 pounds evaporated apples.

    1¼ pounds sugar.

    ¼ ounce cinnamon.

Add the sugar and spice to the stewed apples and mix well. The addition of a few slices of lemon will improve it. Make the pies with a double crust and bake about 20 minutes in a 15-count oven.

The above recipe is sufficient for about seven pies. Nearly any kind of fruit may be substituted for the apples.

Pie, chocolate meringue.
>   1 gallon milk.
>   ¼ ounce salt.
>   8 ounces chocolate.
>   16 ounces flour.
>   24 yolks of eggs,
>   2 pounds sugar.
>   ½ ounce vanilla extract.

Mix seven-eighths of the milk with salt and chocolate and cook in a boiler until smooth on top. Stir the flour into the remaining 1 pint of cold milk and pour this into a double boiler with the hot milk and chocolate. Cook for 8 or 10 minutes, until it thickens, stirring constantly. Now cream the eggs and sugar thoroughly. Pour the hot mixture over the creamed eggs and sugar. Replace in double boiler and cook from 1 to 3 minutes, stirring constantly. Remove from the range and when cool add the vanilla extract.

After the pie crust has been baked to a light brown, fill the crust with the above mixture and cover with a meringue made as follows:

>   24 whites of eggs.
>   ¼ ounce salt.
>   ½ pound sugar, powdered.
>   ¼ ounce vanilla extract.

Add the salt to the eggs and beat with a whip until stiff and flaky; beat the sugar in slowly, then add the vanilla, beating until the froth is stiff. Place on pies with the aid of a smooth knife and brown on upper shelf of a brisk oven. The mixture makes twelve 8-inch pies, and costs about $1.

Pie, cocoanut (1-gallon mixture).
>   20 eggs.
>   1½ pints milk.
>   2½ pounds sugar.
>   ½ ounce extract.
>   ½ pound butter.
>   5 pounds coconut.

Beat the eggs, milk, sugar, and extract together, and add sufficient water to make 1 gallon. Prepare about 12 or 14 single crusts and spread about 6 ounces of coconut in each crust; then pour in the mixture prepared as above, adding to each pie a piece of butter about the size of a walnut. Bake in a 15-count oven about 20 minutes.

Pie, lemon meringue (1-gallon mixture).

    2½ quarts water.

    2 pounds granulated sugar.

    6 to 10 lemons,

    ½ pound butter.

    12 ounces cornstarch.

    16 eggs.

    1 can evaporated milk,

    ½ pound powdered sugar.

Add the juice and rinds of the lemons to the water; boil 5 minutes and remove the rinds; add the sugar and butter; mix the cornstarch in a pint of water and add, stirring in quickly; let come to a boil and remove from the range. Whip the yolks of the eggs and add to them the milk, and sufficient water to make 1 gallon. This mixture is sufficient for eight pies. Take the usual crust, one for each plate; roll out as usual and prick a few times with a fork; bake the crusts until light brown and pour in the mixture. Let stand for a while and beat the whites of the eggs and powdered sugar to a cream. Place about one-fourth inch of the beaten eggs over each pie and coat with granulated sugar if desired. Bake in a 12-count oven about 3 minutes.

Pie, vinegar (1-gallon mixture).

    5 pints water,

    ½ pint vinegar.

    2½ pounds sugar.

    6 eggs.

    10 ounces cornstarch.

Mix the water, vinegar, and sugar and bring to a boil on the range. Dissolve the cornstarch in 1 pint of cold water; then beat up the eggs, adding them to the cornstarch and water. Add the whole to the boiling mixture on the range. Stir well with a wire whip. Cook about 3 minutes and remove from range. There should be sufficient hot water added to the boiling mixture to make 1 gallon. Pie crust must be filled while mixture is hot, same as lemon pies.

This mixture is sufficient for eight pies.

Pie, mince. For each pie use one-third pound of mince-meat and two-thirds liquid. The liquid may be either sugar, sirup, molasses, cider, or a mixture of one-tenth brandy and nine-tenths water. Mix the mince-meat and liquid thoroughly and use a double pie crust; bake about 20 minutes in a 15-count oven.

To make mince-meat.

    5 pounds beef (cooked).

    6 pounds suet.

    20 pounds dried apples.

    10 pounds dried peaches.

    1 pound cinnamon.

    ¼ pound cloves.

    1 ounce black pepper.

    10 pounds sugar.

    1 pound salt.

    10 pounds seeded prunes.

      And, if desired—

    5 pounds currants.

    15 pounds raisins.

    2 pounds candied citron.

    1 pound lemon peel.

    1 pound orange peel.

Run the beef, suet, apples, peaches, and prunes through the meat chopper, each separately; mix with the spices, adding only sufficient water to moisten; pack in a suitable keg that has been thoroughly cleaned. This preparation is suitable for use in garrison or in the field and will keep as long as water is kept from it. Five pounds are sufficient for 15 pies, the above recipe being sufficient for 150 pies.

Pie, pumpkin or squash.

    25 pounds pumpkin.

    6 pounds sugar.

    20 eggs.

    1 nutmeg.

    ⅛ ounce cloves.

    ⅛ ounce ginger.

    1 ounce salt.

    2 cans evaporated milk.

Peel and clean the pumpkin; cut into pieces about 2 ounces each; pour 1 inch of water into a boiler; then put in the pumpkin. One inch of water will be sufficient, even though the boiler be filled with pumpkin, as pumpkin (or squash) contains much water. Boil slowly until done, about 40 minutes. Then mash well, add the beaten eggs, sugar, milk, and spices and mix well; make the pies without a top crust, and bake slowly. This recipe may be improved by the addition of a small amount of cream. Sufficient for about 15 pies.

Pudding, apple (for 60 men).
>   4 pounds apples, diced.
>   16 pounds bread.
>   4 pounds sugar.
>   2 ounces cinnamon.

Stew the apples in 1½ gallons water, slice the bread and toast it; spread the toast in the bottom of a well-greased bake pan; then spread over it a layer of the apples sprinkled with sugar and cinnamon; continue alternate layers of toast and apples until all are used; bake in a quick oven about 20 minutes and serve with a plain or caramel sauce.

Nearly any kind of fresh or dried fruit maybe used and the pudding named accordingly.

Pudding, bread, with sauce (for 60 men).
>   12 pounds bread crusts.
>   2 pounds dried fruit.
>   2 pounds sugar.
>   1 ounce cinnamon.
>   2 cans evaporated milk.
>   6 eggs.

Soak the bread in cold water and squeeze out with the hands; season with sugar and cinnamon; mix well and spread about 1 inch deep in pans; over this spread about 1 inch of stewed fruit; then another layer of the bread; over the top spread sugar and cinnamon; bake about 40 minutes in a medium hot oven. Serve hot or cold with cream sauce. This makes an excellent dish and gives an opportunity to use all the scraps of bread on hand. A better pudding may be made by dipping the bread in milk and not squeezing it out. It will be still further improved by adding eggs.

Pudding, corn starch (for 60 men).

4 pounds sugar.

1 ounce salt.

3 packages corn starch.

4 cans evaporated milk.

1 ounce flavoring extract.

Dissolve the corn starch in about 3 quarts of cold water; add 3 gallons of boiling water, the sugar, salt, and milk. After cooking 5 minutes remove from the range, cool, and add the extract. This pudding is improved by the substitution of milk for water and the addition of about four eggs to each gallon. Pour into vegetable dishes, and when cool set in ice box; serve cold with milk.

Pudding, plum (for 60 men).

2 pounds sugar.

3 pounds dried fruit, chopped fine.

3 pounds beef suet, chopped fine.

1½ ounces salt.

¼ ounce cloves.

1 ounce cinnamon,

¼ nutmeg.

4 ounces baking powder.

6 pounds flour.

Mix the flour, baking powder, salt, beef suet, fruit, and spices in the order named; dissolve the sugar in water and add together with sufficient cold water to make a stiff dough; use 5-pound lard pails or pudding cans and fill each about two-thirds full of the mixture. If no lids are provided, tie a cloth tightly over the top of each pail or can. Place in a boiler containing sufficient boiling water to one-third submerge the pails or cans and maintain the water at about the same height during the process of cooking by the addition of more boiling water when necessary. Boil from five to eight hours. Remove from the cans, split lengthwise through the center, and serve in large vegetable dishes, with a dressing prepared as follows:

Sauce for plum pudding.

1½ pounds sugar.

1 tablespoonful lemon extract.

½ pint vinegar.

1 can evaporated milk.

½ ounce salt.

4 ounces starch or flour.

Dissolve the sugar in 3 quarts of water; let come to a boil and add a batter made of the corn starch or flour and one-half pint of cold water; add the vinegar, milk, extract, and a pinch of soda.

Pudding, rice (for 60 men).
>5 pounds rice.
>15 eggs.
>3 cans evaporated milk.
>5 pounds sugar.
>¼ ounce extract.

Boil the rice for a few minutes and then strain through a sieve; add the eggs, cream, and sugar, with a pinch of salt and sufficient water to cover about one-half inch; bake slowly in the oven until slightly brown. The rice should not be overboiled, as the kernels should remain separate and firm. Serve with cold or hot sauce flavored with lemon.

Pudding, tapioca (for 60 men).
>2 gallons cold water.
>2 pounds tapioca.
>4 pounds sugar.
>2 pounds dried fruit.

Add the water to the tapioca and let simmer on end of range for about two hours; then add the fruit, and if desired, 12 well-beaten eggs. The fruit and the eggs should be beaten into the mixture while hot.

Raisins, currants, or any tart berries or fruit may be used.

SMALL DOUGHS.

Potato yeast (1-gallon mixture).
>4 pounds potatoes.
>2 ounces sugar.
>1 ounce salt.
>4 ounces flour.
>2 ounces dried yeast.

Clean potatoes thoroughly and boil until well done. Place the sugar and flour in a clean wooden or earthen-ware receptacle. Strain the water from the potatoes into another vessel. Place the hot potatoes on top of the sugar and flour, mash them and mix thoroughly.

Add hot potato water, mix well, and set aside to cool. Place dried yeast in 1 pint of cold water and soak. When the mixture is about the temperature of the hand add the dried yeast and sufficient water to make 1 gallon. Mix thoroughly. Set in a temperature of about 85° F. to prove.

This yeast will require approximately 10 hours to mature, depending on the temperature, and if after maturing it is kept in a temperature below 60° F., will keep for several days.

Small dough (1-gallon mixture). *To make the sponge.*—Soak three yeast cakes in a pint of lukewarm water until soft (or use 1 pint of stock yeast prepared in the kitchen) and add two medium-sized potatoes which have been boiled until well done, and add enough lukewarm water to make one-half gallon. Make into a stiff batter, by adding about 6 pounds of flour, and let rise and fall. When it has dropped about 1 inch, add sufficient water to make 1 gallon; make a dough by adding about 8 pounds of flour and the following ingredients:

		Jenny Linds or sweet fruit dough	Plain sweet dough
Salt	ounces	3	3
Sugar	pounds	1½ or 1	¾
Butter, lard or drippings*	do	2, 1½, 1 or ½	½
Eggs*	number	10, 6, or 4	0
Raisins*	pounds	3, 2, or 1	0
Currants*	do	3, 2, or 1	0
Extracts*	ounces	1 or ½	0

* Where two or more quantities are given in the same column, correspondingly large or small amounts should be used together. The richness of the product depends upon the quantities of such ingredients used.

Note.—The temperature of the sponge, of the dough, and of the buns while proving should be as near to 80° F. as possible.

Let the dough rise to about three time its size, punch down, work over and permit to rise to twice its original size. Then work into 1-pound loaves (round), weighing the dough on the scales, and let prove for about 15 or 20 minutes. Then, for small doughs, cut into eight equal parts. This can best be done by rolling the proof ball or loaf, cut into a long cylinder, dividing it in halves with the scraper, subdividing each half into halves, and then in a similar way subdividing again. The above recipe is sufficient for about 180 buns, or about 22 Jenny Linds.

Buns, currant (for 60 men).
   3 pounds currants.
   ¼ pound sugar.
   ½ pound lard.

Prepare a 1-gallon mixture of small dough, using in the dough the ingredients above named in addition to those used in the plain dough mixture. After proving and molding into loaves, divide each loaf into eight equal parts, and round up each piece; place in pan about 1 inch apart; glaze the tops with melted lard; set in a temperature of 80° F.; let rise to twice their size and bake in a medium oven (18-count) for 40 minutes.

Cake, apple (for 60 men).
   12 pounds fresh apples.

Prepare a 1-gallon mixture of sweet dough. After proving and molding, roll out in pieces of about 1 pound each and about 8 inches square; place in the bake pans, peel the apples and cut into very thin slices; place in thin layers over the top; sprinkle with a little cinnamon and sugar; let prove to twice their size, and bake in a 20-count oven about 30 minutes. If desired, a custard consisting of one-third eggs and two-thirds milk, with about 2 pounds of sugar to the gallon, may be poured over the cake before baking.

Kuchen, apple.—Prepare a 1-gallon mixture of sweet dough, molding it into pieces weighing about 1 pound each; let prove to twice their size; roll out three-fourths of the loaves about the size of a pie tin and about one-fourth inch in thickness; put in pie tin and cover with a thin layer of cooked apples, seasoned highly with cinnamon and sugar; then use the remainder of the dough, cut into strips weighing about 1 ounce each, by placing the strips over the fruit, each strip extending entirely across the tin; and press the ends against the dough in the tins so that they will adhere. Bake in a 20-count oven about 30 minutes.

Biscuits (for 60 men).
>10 pounds flour.
>1¼ pounds fat (lard preferred).
>2 ounces sugar.
>2 ounces salt.
>10 ounces baking powder.

Mix the dry ingredients and sift; work in the lard and mix thoroughly; add sufficient water to make a soft dough; roll out about one-half inch thick; cut out with a biscuit cutter and place in bake pan about one-half inch apart; bake in a 12-count oven about 10 minutes; serve hot with butter or sirup.

When using baking powder, use cold water (or milk) and keep in a cool place before baking.

Bread, corn (for 60 men).
>5 pounds corn meal.
>3 pounds flour.
>1½ ounces sugar.
>8 ounces fat (lard or drippings).
>8 ounces baking powder.

Mix the dry ingredients and sift; work in the lard and mix thoroughly; add sufficient water to make a soft dough; spread in bake pans to depth of 2 inches, and bake in a 15-count oven about 40 minutes.

Buns, corn (for 60 men).
>4 pounds corn meal.
>1 quart yeast.
>4 ounces salt.
>½ pound fat.
>1 pint sirup.
>5 quarts water.

Let the water come to a boil and whip the corn meal in slowly to prevent the formation of lumps; let boil for 5 minutes; when cool add the yeast, salt, fat, and sirup; add sufficient flour to make a stiff dough, and handle the same as other yeast preparations.

DRINKS.

Cocoa or chocolate (1 gallon).

  3 to 5 ounces cocoa or chocolate.

  5 ounces sugar.

  4 ounces evaporated milk.

  1 gallon (scant) of water.

Bring the water to a boil, add the cocoa and boil five minutes; add the milk and sugar to taste. Whip slightly with a wire whipper before serving. One gallon is sufficient for from 6 to 10 men. Serve hot.

Coffee (for 60 men).

Coffee is generally served for breakfast and dinner, and should always be prepared fresh at least once a day.

The following method is suggested:

Breakfast: Put 7½ gallons of water in the boiler and let come to a boil; add 2¼ pounds roasted and ground coffee, and remove from the range immediately. Allow to stand 15 minutes; add 1 pint of cold water, and allow to stand a few minutes longer before serving. To sweeten, add 4 or 5 ounces of sugar to each gallon.

Dinner: Allow the grounds to remain in the boiler after breakfast and add sufficient water to make 7½ gallons; allow to come to a boil and add 3 ounces of coffee, roasted and ground, for each gallon of fresh water used; remove from the range and allow to stand 15 minutes; add a pint of cold water, and allow to stand a few minutes before serving.

Coffee should be made for immediate use only.

To parch or roast coffee: Place about 10 pounds of green coffee in a bake pan and set in a brisk oven, leaving the door on the first notch until the coffee is thoroughly dried. Close the oven and stir frequently with a spoon until nicely browned.

Lemonade (for 60 men).

  7½ gallons ice water.

  4 pounds sugar.

  60 lemons.

Squeeze the juice from the lemons with a lemon squeezer and add to the water; sweeten to taste and stir thoroughly before serving. Serve ice cold.

Tea (for 60 men).
> 7½ gallons fresh water.
> 3½ ounces good tea.

Allow the water to come to a boil; remove from range; suspend the tea from the top of the boiler in a muslin cloth and allow to stand in the boiling water for five minutes. The cloth should be sufficiently large to give the tea plenty of room, so that the boiling water will penetrate all portions of it. Remove the leaves and serve immediately.

Iced tea: Using 2 gallons of water and 5 ounces of tea; prepare as in the preceding recipe. Just before serving, add sufficient cold water to make 10 gallons. The juice of a dozen lemons may be added, if desired.

To sweeten tea, add about 4 ounces of sugar to each gallon of tea.

BIBLIOGRAPHY

OFFICIAL PUBLICATIONS

J. C. Calhoun, "Reduction of the Army Considered" Communicated to the House of Representatives, December 14, 1818, in *No. 168 American State Papers: Documents, Legislative and Executive, of the Congress of the United States* (Washington, 1832), Class V. Military Affairs, 779–782.

General Regulation for the Army (1821).

Revised United States Army Regulations of 1861 (U.S. Government Printing Office, 1863).

War Department, Commissary of Subsistence, Capt James M. Sanderson, Camp Fires and Camp Cooking or Culinary Hints for the Soldier (HQ Army of the Potomac, Washington, 1862).

War Department, Office Commissary General of Subsistence, *Manual for Army Cooks,* Document No. 18 (Washington, 1896).

War Department, Office of the Commissary-General, *Manual for the Subsistence Department, United States Army* (Washington, 1910).

War Department, Office of the Quartermaster General, *Manual for Army Cooks*, Document No. 564 (Washington, 1916).

War Department, Surgeon-General's Office, *Report on the Hygiene of the United States Army* (Washington, 1872).

OTHER PUBLICATIONS QUOTED OR CONSULTED

J. W. Barriger, 'Subsistence Department', in T. F. Rodenbough and W. L. Haskin (eds.), *The Army of the United States: Historical Sketches of Staff and Line with Portraits of Generals-in-Chief* (New York: Maynard, Merrill & Co., 1896), 67–82.

General Chaffee, "Report on the China Relief Expedition, 1900," in The War Department, *Five Years of the War Department Following the War With Spain, 1899–1903* (Washington, D. C., 1904), 395–407.

William C. Davis, *A Taste for War: The Culinary History of the Blue and Gray* ((Lincoln: University of Nebraska Press, 2011).

E. N. Horsford, *The Army Ration: How to Diminish its Weight and Bulk, Secure Economy in its Administration, Avoid Waste, and Increase the Comfort, Efficiency, and Mobility of Troops* (D. Van Nostram, 1864).

Brigadier-General Henry G. Sharpe (revised by Captain Frank A. Cook), *The Provisioning of the Modern Army in the Field* (Franklin Hudson Publishing Co., 1909).